# WESTWARD EXPANSION

**INTERPRETING PRIMARY DOCUMENTS**

James D. Torr, Book Editor

Daniel Leone, President
Bonnie Szumski, Publisher
Scott Barbour, Managing Editor

**GREENHAVEN PRESS ®**

**THOMSON**
**GALE**
Tulare County Library

San Diego • Detroit • New York • San Francisco • Cleveland
New Haven, Conn. • Waterville, Maine • London • Munich

© 2003 by Greenhaven Press. Greenhaven Press is an imprint of The Gale Group, Inc., a division of Thomson Learning, Inc.

Greenhaven® and Thomson Learning™ are trademarks used herein under license.

*For more information, contact*
Greenhaven Press
27500 Drake Rd.
Farmington Hills, MI 48331-3535
Or you can visit our Internet site at http://www.gale.com

Cover credit: © Mary Evans Picture Library

**LIBRARY OF CONGRESS CATALOGING-IN-PUBLICATION DATA**

Westward expansion / by James D. Torr, book editor.
    p. cm. — (Interpreting American history through primary documents series)
Includes bibliographical references and index.
ISBN 0-7377-1133-7 (pbk. : alk. paper) —
ISBN 0-7377-1134-5 (hardback : alk. paper)
    1. West (U.S.)—Discovery and exploration—Sources—Juvenile literature.
2. West (U.S.)—History—Sources—Juvenile literature. 3. Frontier and pioneer life—West (U.S.)—Sources—Juvenile literature. 4. Indians of North America—West (U.S.)—History—Sources—Juvenile literature. 5. Indians of North America—Government relations—Sources—Juvenile literature. 6. United States—Territorial expansion—Sources—Juvenile literature. [1. West (U.S.)—Discovery and exploration—Sources. 2. West (U.S.)—History—Sources. 3. Frontier and pioneer life—West (U.S.)—Sources. 4. Indians of North America—West (U.S.)—History—Sources. 5. Indians of North America—Government relations—Sources. 6. United States—Territorial expansion—Sources.] I. Torr, James D., 1974– . II. Series.
F591 .W64 2003
978'.01—dc21                                                                    2002000499

Printed in the United States of America

# CONTENTS

## Chapter 1: The Lure of the West

# Chapter 2: Conquest of Native America

gathering of Sioux and other tribes that (unbeknown to Custer) was over three thousand strong.

# Chapter 3: Manifest Destiny

Mexico, as well as the concern that Texas would enter the Union as a slave state.

# Chapter 4: The Western Railroads

and in doing so, put an end to many Plains Indians' traditional way of life.

# FOREWORD

In a debate on the nature of the historian's task, the Canadian intellectual Michael Ignatieff wrote, "I don't think history is a lesson in patriotism. It should be a lesson in truth. And the truth is both painful and many-sided." Part of Ignatieff's point was that those who seek to understand the past should guard against letting prejudice or patriotism interfere with the truth. This point, although simple, is subtle. Everyone would agree that patriotism is no excuse for outright fabrication, and that prejudice should never induce a historian to deliberately lie or deceive. Ignatieff's concern, however, was not so much with deliberate falsification as it was with the way prejudice and patriotism can lead to selective perception, which can skew the judgment of even those who are sincere in their efforts to understand the past. The truth, especially about the how and why of historical events, is seldom simple, and those who wish to genuinely understand the past must be sensitive to its complexities.

Each of the anthologies in the Greenhaven Press Interpreting Primary Documents series strives to portray the events and attitudes of the past in all their complexity. Rather than providing a simple narrative of the events, each volume presents a variety of views on the issues and events under discussion and encourages the student to confront and examine the complexity that attends the genuine study of history.

Furthermore, instead of aiming simply to transmit information from historian to student, the series is designed to develop and train students to become historians themselves, by focusing on the interpretation of primary documents. Such documents, including newspaper articles, speeches, personal reflections, letters, diaries, memoranda, and official reports, are the raw material from which the historian refines an authentic understanding of the past. The anthology examining desegregation, for instance, includes the voices of presidents, state governors, and ordinary citizens, and draws from the *Congressional Record,* newspapers and magazines, letters, and books published at the time. The selections differ in scope and opinion as well, allowing the student to examine the issue of desegregation from a variety of perspectives. By looking frankly at the arguments offered by those in favor of racial segregation and by those opposed, for example, students can better understand those arguments, the people who advanced them, and the time in which they lived.

The structure of each book in the Interpreting Primary Documents series helps readers sharpen the critical faculties the serious study of history requires. A concise introduction outlines the era or event at hand and provides the necessary historical background. The chapters themselves begin with a preface containing a straightforward account of the events discussed and an overview of how these events can be interpreted in different ways by examining the different documents in the chapter. The selections, in turn, are chosen for their accessibility and relevance, and each is preceded by a short introduction offering historical context and a summary of the author's point of view. A set of questions to guide interpretation accompanies each article and encourages readers to examine the authors' prejudices, probe their assumptions, and compare and contrast the various perspectives offered in the chapter. Finally, a detailed timeline traces the development of key events, a comprehensive bibliography of selected secondary material guides further research, and a thorough index lets the reader quickly access relevant information.

As Ignatieff remarked, in the same debate in which he urged the historian to favor truth over blind patriotism, "History for me is the study of arguments." The Interpreting Primary Documents series is for readers eager to understand the arguments, and attitudes, that animated historical change.

# INTRODUCTION

America's westward expansion is often viewed as a testament to the pioneer spirit. In this interpretation, the nation's growth is attributed to the countless individual settlers who built the communities of the West. Frontier farmers, miners, ranchers, and merchants proved that America was indeed the "land of opportunity," where people could make new lives for themselves through courage and hard work. However, America's westward expansion can also be seen as the result of organized conquest—not just of the western frontier but also of the people who inhabited it. Westward expansion was marked by war with Native American tribes and with Mexico as well as by the threat of war with Great Britain and other European powers.

Both interpretations of westward expansion have their merits, as do others. Individualism and conquest were both major themes in the westward movement, as were greed, racism, adventure, and hope. Furthermore, westward expansion was composed of many smaller events, such as the Lewis and Clark expedition, the removal of the eastern Indians, the California gold rush, the Mexican War, the war with the Plains Indians, and the building of the transcontinental railroad. Each of these played out a theme of westward expansion and became one facet in the larger story of settling the West. The differing interpretations of the legacy and the significance of each of these events makes westward expansion one of the most interesting and controversial aspects of U.S. history.

## East of the Mississippi

Westward expansion did not become a national passion until the nineteenth century, but as frontier historian Ray Allen Billington notes, settlement of the American frontier "was a process that was repeated over and over again for three hundred years—between the first settlements at James Town and Plymouth and Massachusetts Bay in the early seventeenth century, to the exhaustion of the public domain in the twentieth."[1] Long before the United States declared its independence from Great Britain, settlers were moving west from the most populous regions of the thirteen colonies into what are now the states of Vermont, Kentucky, Tennessee, and Ohio. One eighteenth-century traveler, in describing the motivations for migration west from his native New England, provided an apt summary of most pioneers:

> Those, who are first inclined to emigrate, are usually such, as have met with difficulties at home. These are commonly joined by persons, who, having large families and small farms, are induced, for the sake of settling their children comfortably, to seek for new and cheaper lands. To both are always added the discontented, the enterprising, the ambitious, and the covetous. . . . Not a small number are influenced by brilliant stories, which everywhere are told concerning most tracts during the early progress of their settlement.[2]

Vermont, Kentucky, and Tennessee in the 1790s, and Ohio in 1803, were the first states to join the Union as the result of the early western migration.

The movement of settlers into the Ohio River Valley initially created problems for the fledgling U.S. government. Much of this territory was inhabited by American Indians who did not want white settlers overrunning their lands. When Thomas Jefferson assumed the presidency in 1801, he was very concerned about this "Indian problem," as it was called at the time. Jefferson hoped that over time the Indians would become "civilized" and assimilated into white culture. However, he also proposed a secondary solution: If certain tribes wanted to maintain their own lands and "savage" culture, he reasoned, they should move farther west, beyond the Mississippi River, where few whites had settled. Jefferson even went as far as suggesting a constitutional amendment guaranteeing Indians' rights to land in the West, but this idea was quickly dropped. Indian removal eventually became official U.S. policy in 1830, after U.S. leaders had committed to conquering the West. But at the dawn of the eighteenth century, European claims to the lands beyond U.S. borders posed far more formidable obstacles to U.S. expansion.

## The Opening of the West

In the South, Spain controlled Florida and Mexico, which at the time included both Texas and much of California. France had claimed the Louisiana Territory—roughly defined as the area between the Mississippi River and the Rocky Mountains, north of Texas, and south of the Columbia River—but had transferred its claim on the territory to Spain in 1762. In the North, Great Britain controlled Canada and much of present-day Oregon and was supporting the Indians of the Great Lakes region in their efforts to maintain control of their lands. Most Federalists (members of the dominant political party in America at the time) felt that these vast territories would be ungovernable, and that obtaining them was not worth provoking war with a European power.

Jefferson, however, was very interested in the West. He envisioned the United States as an "empire of liberty" that would one day span the continent. During the eighteenth century little was known of the geography west of the Mississippi, and even less of the regions beyond the Missouri River. "This was to change, however," writes historian Gerald F. Kreyche, "for President Thomas Jefferson had an unquenchable yearning for such knowledge."[3] Jefferson made preliminary plans for an expedition to explore the West as early as 1784, but he was unable to implement them until after he was elected president.

In 1800, in a secret treaty, Spain agreed to return Louisiana to France. When rumors of the agreement reached

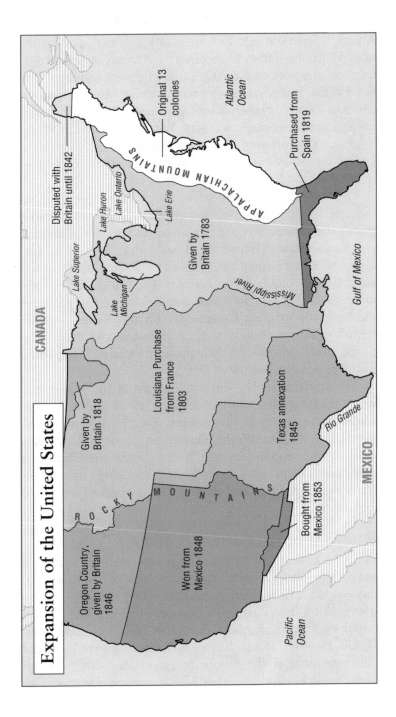

Expansion of the United States

Original 13 colonies

Disputed with Britain until 1842

Atlantic Ocean

Purchased from Spain 1819

APPALACHIAN MOUNTAINS

Lake Superior

Lake Huron

Lake Ontario

Lake Erie

Given by Britain 1783

Lake Michigan

Gulf of Mexico

Mississippi River

CANADA

Given by Britain 1818

Louisiana Purchase from France 1803

Texas annexation 1845

Rio Grande

ROCKY MOUNTAINS

Oregon Country, given by Britain 1846

Won from Mexico 1848

Bought from Mexico 1853

MEXICO

Pacific Ocean

America, Jefferson sent Revolutionary War hero and governor of Virginia, James Monroe to Paris to negotiate the purchase of the port of New Orleans. In a very fortunate (for the United States) turn of events, while Monroe was en route to France, French leader Napoléon Bonaparte began preparing for a possible war with England. In need of funds, the French negotiators offered to sell the United States all of Louisiana for, as Kreyche puts it, "an even then paltry sum of approximately fifteen million dollars."[4]

The serendipitous Louisiana Purchase nearly doubled the size of the nation, and it allowed Jefferson to make public the exploratory expedition he had been planning for years. Captains Meriwether Lewis and William Clark, along with over forty other soldiers, started up the Missouri River from St. Louis on May 14, 1804. One of their main goals was to find an all-water route to the Pacific—the fabled Northwest Passage. In this they failed, but the wealth of information they did accumulate and the reports of the lands they saw on their journey signaled the opening of the previously unknown West.

As important as the settlements east of the Mississippi were, the Lewis and Clark expedition, more than any other single event, marked the beginning of westward movement. For the rest of the nineteenth century, Americans worked to conquer the frontier that Lewis and Clark had traversed. Lewis and Clark's journey has come to symbolize both the positive and the negative aspects of westward expansion.

## Removal of the Eastern Indians

One of the most controversial aspects of the new westward movement—both during the nineteenth century and today—was the U.S. government's treatment of American Indians. Although hostilities between Indians and whites dated back to the earliest European colonies in the New World, the 1830 Indian Removal Act, which gave President Andrew Jackson the power to negotiate with tribes to move west beyond the Mississippi, marked an important shift in U.S. Indian policy. Indian-white relations had been characterized by racism and broken treaties in the past, but among leaders such as Thomas Jefferson and his predecessors there had always been at least the hope that the Indians would someday embrace American institutions and culture. In contrast, Jackson asserted that Indians had "neither the intelligence, the industry, the moral habits, nor the desire of improvement"[5] to live among whites. According to historian Richard White, "Removal made it clear that there was no room for a common world that included independent Indians living with whites."[6]

The Indian Removal Act established a "permanent" Indian Territory in what is now Oklahoma, in which whites would not be allowed to settle. President Jackson insisted that Indian removal was for the benefit of the eastern tribes and would be completely voluntary. In an 1835 letter to the Cherokee, who were refusing to leave their lands in Georgia and other southern states, Jackson wrote,

> I am seriously desirous to promote your welfare. Listen to me, therefore, while I tell you that you cannot remain where you now are. Circumstances that cannot be controlled . . . render it impossible that you can flourish in a civilized community. You have but one remedy within your reach. And that is, to remove to the West and join your countrymen, who are already established there. And the sooner you do this, the sooner you will commence your career of improvement and prosperity.[7]

Although Indian removal was supposedly voluntary, Jackson's letter was effectively an ultimatum. When the Cherokee still refused to leave, they were forcibly marched west. On the Trail of Tears, writes White, "one in eight Cherokees died on their way to, or shortly after arriving in, the Indian Territory."[8]

Indian removal was a very controversial policy in its time. Among those who opposed the policy were congressman Henry Clay, frontiersman and politician Davy Crockett, and orator and statesman Daniel Webster. In support of the policy were the thousands of settlers who occupied former Indian lands. Though billed as a solution to the conflict between Indians and whites, Indian removal ultimately failed in this regard. Once the eastern Indians' former lands were taken, settlers ventured beyond the Mississippi. But for a few years, at least, most whites found it easier to settle outside the Indian Territory.

## Oregon and Texas

During the mid-1840s settlers heading west hurdled the Indian reservations of the Great Plains, following the Oregon Trail across the continent to the Pacific Northwest. As Gregory M. Franzwa, author of *The Oregon Trail Revisited*, explains, "Interest in the Pacific Northwest, which had begun to build with the 1806 return of Lewis and Clark from their famous expedition to the region, continued to grow with the tales of fur traders, missionaries, and adventurers during the next thirty-five years."[9] Rising land prices during the late 1830s prompted a few dozen pioneers to brave the Oregon Trail in 1841, and at least 125 more followed in 1842. Then, writes Franzwa, "During the hard winter of 1842–43, interest in overland migration surged as thousands of midwestern farmers attended meetings of emigration societies to learn more about the two-thousand-mile trail and the lush valley to which it led."[10] The result was the great migration of 1843, in which some two thousand emigrants made the trek to Oregon. Thousands more followed over the next few years. "Oregon fever" had swept the nation.

As with most aspects of westward expansion, Oregon fever was not embraced by all Americans. Under the 1818 Treaty of Joint Occupation, the United States had agreed to share part of Oregon with England. The English hoped that eventually the area south of the Columbia River would become U.S. territory, while the region north of the forty-ninth parallel would remain British. But as American pioneers flooded the Willamette Valley, many U.S. leaders—particularly Democrats, who favored expansion—began clamoring for "All Oregon or None." They hoped that American occupation of Oregon would eventually lead to rich commerce with the Orient—something Americans had dreamed of ever since Lewis and Clark first set out in search of the fabled Northwest Passage. Democratic senator Stephen A. Douglas proclaimed that "the great point of issue [in the dispute with England over Oregon was] the freedom of the Pacific Ocean, . . . the trade of China, of Japan, of the East Indies, and . . . maritime ascendancy."[11] Democrats were opposed by Whigs, who worried that the growing controversy over Oregon could lead to another war with England, or at least severely damage U.S.-British relations.

The threat of war also loomed in the South. Americans had been settling in the Mexican territory of Texas since the 1820s. In 1836 Texas had declared its independence from Mexico, but the Mexican government still maintained that Texas was a Mexican territory. Just as pressure was mounting on the U.S. government to lay claim to Oregon, Democrats also began arguing that the United States should annex the Republic of Texas—even though doing so would probably lead to war with Mexico. In addition to a split between Democrats and Whigs over whether war with Mexico was justified, annexation of Texas was tied to the divisive issue of slavery. Southerners tended to favor annexation, and northerners opposed it because they did not want another slave state admitted to the Union.

## Manifest Destiny

Both Oregon and Texas became key issues in the 1844 presidential election. Democratic candidate James K. Polk ran his entire campaign on a platform of expansion. "I have *no hesitation* in declaring that I am in favor of the Immediate Re-Annexation of Texas,"[12] he declared, and in regard to Oregon his slogan was "54°40' or fight!" (in reference to the parallel at the southern tip of Alaska that

Democrats felt should be the northern border of American-occupied Oregon). Polk's Whig opponent, Henry Clay, was ardently opposed to the annexation of Texas and ignored the issue in his campaign.

Polk's victory in the 1844 election (even though it was hardly a landslide) seemed to indicate that public support for westward expansion had reached a new high. Expansionists argued more forcefully then ever that the United States had a duty to repel the English institution of monarchy from North American soil and to bring freedom and democracy to the people of Texas. According to Ray Allen Billington, "One more thing was needed before this exuberant belief could be translated into action: a catchy phrase that would sum up the Americans' faith in themselves."[13] That phrase came in the summer of 1845, when John L. O'Sullivan, editor of the *Democratic Review*, proclaimed America's "manifest destiny to overspread the continent allotted by Providence for the free development of our yearly multiplying millions."[14] The phrase *Manifest Destiny*, which suggests that westward expansion was a natural, justified, and inevitable process, was quickly taken up by expansionists.

Manifest Destiny was interpreted in a variety of ways during the 1840s, and there were several components to Americans' faith in this doctrine. Some were attracted to the religious overtones of Manifest Destiny—the belief that it was God's will that Americans spread over the entire continent. For others, the doctrine was simply a new and eloquent way of expressing Americans' longstanding belief that their own ideas about liberty, freedom, and democracy were superior and would eventually be adopted worldwide. As Sanford Wexler puts it, "Americans believed their democratic institutions so perfect that no boundaries could contain them."[15]

Finally, there was an element of racism in Manifest Destiny. As historian Reginald Horsman argues, by the 1840s Americans had convinced themselves that "the failure of the Indians to benefit from the American advance had stemmed from their inherent inferiority."[16] In this view it was the Indians' own fault, and not the United States', that they had been overrun by white settlers. Appeals to Manifest Destiny were used to retroactively justify the removal of the eastern Indians and the harm it caused them as well as to justify the government's ongoing conflicts with various Indian tribes. Manifest Destiny as a doctrine of racial superiority was also applied to Mexicans: "The Mexicans are *aboriginal Indians*," one newspaper proclaimed, "and they must share the destiny of their race."[17] In this way Manifest Destiny was used to justify war with Mexico.

## The Mexican War

Even before Polk was inaugurated, lame-duck president John Tyler, with Congress's approval, had extended an offer of annexation to the Republic of Texas. President Polk acted swiftly to ensure that Texas accepted the offer, and in December 1845 Texas became the twenty-eighth state. Mexico immediately severed diplomatic ties with the United States. War seemed imminent.

While tensions were rising over Texas, the British became concerned even more about American designs on Oregon. Polk was aware that the United States could not afford to provoke both Mexico and Great Britain, so in a swift series of diplomatic maneuvers he demanded a U.S. boundary of 54°40' in Oregon. When the British ambassador refused, Polk "settled" for a boundary at the 49th parallel and for congressional nullification of the Treaty of Joint Occupation, thus refuting the British claim to the region.

Flush with this diplomatic victory, Polk again turned his attention to Texas. The Polk administration insisted that the Texas it had annexed stretched all the way down to the Rio Grande—even though the Republic of Texas had its border at the Nueces River, approximately 150 miles north of the Rio Grande. This angered Mexico even further. Polk may have had an ulterior motive in pursuing this border dispute. Having secured Oregon, Polk was afraid that Great Britain might steal a portion of California away from

Mexico if he did not act first. Polk sent a special envoy, John Slidell, both to negotiate the border dispute and to offer Mexico $40 million for California. But he also sent U.S. troops past the Nueces. Historians William F. Deverell and Anne F. Hyde summarize the historic result:

> With Mexicans already angry over annexation of the Republic of Texas, Polk sent a delegation to Mexico City to buy California and New Mexico. At the same time, he sent four thousand troops into the disputed border area, actively provoking war with Mexico. Tension mounted as Mexican and United States troops stared at each other across the Rio Grande. The inevitable happened: the troops fired on each other and President Polk immediately declared war [on May 11, 1846].[18]

The Mexican War, and particularly the events that precipitated its outbreak, were very controversial at the time. Editor Horace Greeley proclaimed the *New York Tribune*'s "open and fearless hostility . . . to the atrocious war waged upon Mexico."[19] Abraham Lincoln, then a Whig congressman from Illinois, demanded to know the exact spot where Mexico had allegedly invaded the United States (as Polk claimed in his war declaration), thereby earning himself the nickname "spotty Lincoln." Abolitionists feared that the United States would conquer all of Mexico and create a new empire for slavery. And virtually the entire Mexican nation decried what it viewed as American imperialism.

Yet despite much criticism, the United States waged war on Mexico for eighteen months. Approximately thirteen thousand Americans and fifty thousand Mexicans lost their lives. Finally, in September 1847, U.S. troops occupied Mexico City and Mexican president Santa Anna issued a surrender. Some ardent expansionists argued that America's Manifest Destiny was to annex all of Mexico. Instead, under the Treaty of Guadalupe-Hidalgo, signed February 2, 1848, Mexico accepted the Rio Grande boundary for

Texas and, for $15 million in payments, ceded all of California and New Mexico to the United States. This was the United States' largest land acquisition since the Louisiana Purchase. As Wexler explains, "The United States gained 1.2 million acres, virtually doubling the size of its territory."[20] Except for the Gadsden Purchase of 1853, in which the United States also acquired much of present-day New Mexico and Arizona for $10 million, the boundaries of the contiguous United States were complete.

## Developing the West

"The victorious conclusion of the Mexican War and its repercussions in Europe seemed to herald the dawn of a new golden age," writes University of Illinois professor Robert W. Johannsen, "golden, in fact, for gold was discovered in California at the very moment California became part of the United States."[21] In January 1848—mere days before the signing of the Treaty of Guadalupe-Hidalgo—John Sutter discovered gold at his mill near Sacramento.

The gold rush that followed was the beginning of an enormous transformation of the West. In 1849 and 1850 over one hundred thousand people flocked to the Pacific Coast. These so-called Argonauts came seeking instant fortune, but the vast majority of them were disappointed. As writer Richard Reinhardt explains,

> Most of the few who profited from the gold rush did so by selling barrels of whiskey, kegs of nails, cords of lumber, bags of flour, bottles of ipecac and liniment and India tonic, portable houses made in Baltimore, tombstones carved in Philadelphia, porter brewed in New York, sherry blended in Spain. They got rich by buying Mexican land cheap and selling it dear or by stealing it from Indians, by opening banks and stage lines and steamboat services, by running saloons, whorehouses, gambling halls, boardinghouses, beer gardens, or private mints.[22]

Thus, although the California gold rush made only a relatively few people rich, it contributed immensely to the development of San Francisco as a city and to California as a state. This process was repeated again and again as other mineral strikes were made throughout the West. Gold was discovered at Pike's Peak, Colorado, in 1858, and silver was found at the Comstock Lode near Virginia City, Nevada, in 1859. Other mineral strikes were made in Idaho, Montana, and Arizona during the late 1850s and early 1860s; in Arizona, Colorado, and the Black Hills of the Dakota Territory during the 1870s; and in Alaska (which was purchased from Russia in 1867) during the 1890s.

## War Against Native America

However, as historian Martin Ridge notes, "The mining frontier, regardless of what was sought—gold, silver, copper, or oil—produced winners and losers. . . . As in all of the American past, but perhaps more so as the result of the mineral frontier, Native Americans lost the most."[23] Many ethnic groups—notably the thousands of Chinese who rushed to the gold mines—experienced discrimination and intolerance during the gold rush, but none fared worse than the California Indians. "The fate of the California Indians constitutes one of the darkest chapters in American history,"[24] writes W. Eugene Hollon in *Frontier Violence: Another Look*. The California Indians experienced disease, enslavement in the mines, and outright massacre at the hands of whites.

The hardships that befell the tribes of the Great Plains, the Southwest, and the Pacific Northwest were less sudden but similarly tragic. From the 1850s through the 1890s more and more white settlers arrived in the West in search of mineral wealth or, as in decades past, cheap land. As whites encroached on Indian lands, hostilities erupted—just as they had east of the Mississippi during the 1820s and 1830s. But now there were no more unwanted western lands for the Indians to move to, so the government forced tribes onto reservation lands that whites did not want. Many tribes resisted, and as a result, more battles occurred between Indians and U.S. troops between 1860 and 1890 than in any other period in U.S. history.

U.S. Indian policy was hotly debated throughout the nineteenth century. Many Americans, particularly those settlers who lived in fear of Indian raids, agreed with General Philip Sheridan's infamous remark that "the only good Indians I ever saw were dead."[25] Yet many Americans condemned the government's treatment of the Indians as barbarous and—given the numerous peace treaties the government had signed with various tribes over the decades—dishonorable. As early as 1869 a special commission reported to President Ulysses S. Grant that "the history of the border white man's connection with the Indian is a sickening record of murder, outrage, robbing, and wrongs committed by the former, as a rule, and occasional savage outbreaks and unspeakable barbarous deeds of retaliation by the latter, as the exception."[26] The views of the Indians themselves were usually ignored. Only after their tribes were decimated and no longer posed a threat were the arguments and pleas of Indian chiefs such as Red Cloud, Black Kettle, Joseph, Seattle, and Sitting Bull paid any heed.

## The Transcontinental Railroad

The completion of the first transcontinental railroad in 1869 marked the beginning of the end of the western Indians' traditional way of life. First, the railroad brought more settlers west than ever before. Second, the railroad brought hunters who destroyed the vast buffalo herds that once roamed the Great Plains. Over 10 million bison were killed during the early 1870s alone, and by 1883 the species was all but extinct. As White explains, "The elimination of the buffalo by white hide hunters cut the heart from the Plains Indian economy. Various military commanders encouraged the slaughter of bison for precisely this reason. Without the buffalo, Plains Indians could not effectively resist American expansion."[27]

As with other stages of westward expansion, one group's loss was another group's gain: Although the transcontinental railroad had tragic consequences for the Plains Indians, it opened up new era of westward migration. "The West could hardly have been settled to any degree of completion without the railroad," writes former Brigham Young University historian Leonard J. Arrington. He notes that within twenty years of the completion of the transcontinental railroad, the population of Nebraska rose from just over 100,000 to more than 1 million, and that of the Dakotas rose from 15,000 to more than 500,000. "More than any other single agency," he maintains, "the railroad converted a nation of diverse sections into 'one nation, indivisible.'"[28]

The transcontinental railroad also opened up a new world of opportunities for western pioneers. It gave birth to the cattle kingdoms, as ranchers in Texas began employing cowboys to drive their herds up the Chisholm Trail or the Goodnight-Loving Trail to towns like Abilene, Wichita, and Dodge City in Kansas, and later Laramie and Miles City in Wyoming. These sometimes unruly "cowtowns" originated the image of the "wild" West that eventually became a staple of popular novels and films. Yet the era of the long drive was short-lived. As historians T. Harry Williams, Richard N. Current, and Frank Freidel explain, "The railroads gave the cattle kingdom access to markets and thus brought it into being; then they destroyed it by bringing the farmers' frontier to the plains."[29] By the 1880s, the open range of the cowboys had been fenced off for crops.

Ray Allen Billington notes that "between 1870 and 1890 more land was occupied and more land placed under cultivation than in all the nation's previous history."[30] The ease of railroad travel was the primary reason so many people went west in this period, but another major draw was the promise of free land. Under the Homestead Act of 1862, all heads of families and males over age twenty-one could claim 160 acres of the public domain, provided they cultivated the land for five years. The homestead movement culminated in 1889, when the government opened 2 million acres in Oklahoma—the last major remnant of the Indian Territory created in 1830—to settlers.

# A Mixed Legacy

After the U.S. census of 1890, the federal government declared that the western frontier had been settled. This was an oversimplification since there were (and still are) many uninhabited areas throughout the West. And the United States had yet to experience its final burst of expansion: In 1898 the United States not only annexed Hawaii, it also went to war with Spain over the independence of Cuba and ended up acquiring Guam, Puerto Rico, and (briefly) the Philippines. But by 1890 the most important goal of westward expansion had been accomplished—America had achieved its Manifest Destiny and "overspread the continent allotted by Providence."

Debate over the legacy of westward expansion began as soon as this expansion was thought to have ended. During the 1890s historian Frederick Jackson Turner began promoting his groundbreaking "frontier thesis," in which he argued that the importance of westward expansion had been grossly underestimated in traditional studies of U.S. history. "American history has been in large degree a history of the colonization of the Great West,"[31] he wrote. Turner placed great emphasis on the individual pioneers who settled the West, arguing, for example, that their willingness to work hard and take risks gave rise to modern Americans' skill as entrepreneurs. Turner's views were further refined by western historians such as Ray Allen Billington.

Many scholars have challenged this individualist vision of westward expansion. They argue that although the pioneer spirit was important, westward expansion was in large part the result of diplomacy (for example, in the Louisiana Purchase and the acquisition of Oregon) and war (against American Indians and Mexico). Richard White, for example, in his 1991 book *"It's Your Misfortune and None of My Own": A History of the American West*, argues that "the American West, more than any other section of the United States, is a creation not so much of individual or local efforts, but of federal efforts. . . . The armies of the federal government conquered the region

[and] agents of the federal government explored it."[32]

The question of whether westward expansion should be interpreted primarily as the result of pioneer heroism or of violent conquest is an important one, because it affects how Americans view their nation. The many controversial aspects of westward expansion are a major part of what makes the nineteenth century such an engaging historical period, and they ensure that the events of the westward movement are always open to new and diverse interpretations.

# Notes

1. Ray Allen Billington, *Westward to the Pacific: An Overview of America's Westward Expansion*. St. Louis, MO: Jefferson National Expansion Historical Association, 1979, p. 7.

2. Quoted in Ray Allen Billington, *Westward Expansion: A History of the American Frontier*. New York: Macmillan, 1967, p. 9.

3. Gerald F. Kreyche, "Lewis and Clark: Trailblazers Who Opened a Continent," *USA Today*, January 1998, p. 23.

4. Gerald F. Kreyche, *Visions of the American West*. Lexington: University of Kentucky Press, 1989, p. 9.

5. Quoted in Richard White, *"It's Your Misfortune and None of My Own": A History of the American West*. Norman: University of Oklahoma Press, 1991, p. 89.

6. White, *"It's Your Misfortune and None of My Own,"* p. 87.

7. Quoted in John Ehle, *Trail of Tears: The Rise and Fall of the Cherokee Nation*. New York: Doubleday, 1988, p. 276.

8. White, *"It's Your Misfortune and None of My Own,"* p. 87.

9. Gregory M. Franzwa, "The Great Migration," *American History Illustrated*, Spring 1993, p. 29.

10. Franzwa, "The Great Migration," p. 30.

11. Quoted in White, *"It's Your Misfortune and None of My Own,"* p. 75.

12. Quoted in Ray Allen Billington, *The Far Western Frontier, 1830–1860*. New York: Harper & Row, 1956, p. 144.

13. Billington, *The Far Western Frontier, 1830–1860,* p. 149.

14. John L. O'Sullivan, "Annexation," *United States Magazine and Democratic Review,* July/August 1845, p. 111.

15. Sanford Wexler, ed., *Westward Expansion: An Eyewitness History*. New York: Facts On File, 1991, p. 141.

16. Reginald Horsman, "American Indian Policy and the Origins of Manifest Destiny," *University of Birmingham Historical Journal*, vol. 10, no. 2, 1968, p. 138.

17. Quoted in Horsman, "American Indian Policy and the Origins of Manifest Destiny," p. 139.

18. William F. Deverell and Anne F. Hyde, eds., *The West in the History of the Nation: A Reader, Volume One: To 1877*. Boston: Bedford/St. Martin's, 2000, pp. 222–23.

19. Quoted in Joseph Shattan, "One-Term Wonder," *American Spectator*, October 1996, p. 35.

20. Wexler, *Westward Expansion*, p. 223.

21. Robert W. Johannsen, "The Mexican War," *Wilson Quarterly*, Spring 1996, p. 107.

22. Richard Reinhardt, "All That Glittered," *American Heritage*, February/March 1998, p. 46.

23. Martin Ridge, "The Legacy of the Gold Rush," *Montana: The Magazine of Western History*, Winter 2000, p. 61.

24. W. Eugene Hollon, *Frontier Violence: Another Look*. New York: Oxford University Press, 1974, p. 61.

25. Quoted in Dee Brown, *Bury My Heart at Wounded Knee: An Indian History of the American West*. New York: Holt, Rinehart, and Winston, 1970, p. 170.

26. Quoted in Hollon, *Frontier Violence*, p. 125.

27. White, *"It's Your Misfortune and None of My Own,"* p. 219.

28. Leonard J. Arrington, "The Transcontinental Railroad and the Development of the West," *Utah Historical Quarterly*, Winter 1969, p. 4.

29. T. Harry Williams, Richard N. Current, and Frank Freidel, *A History of the United States (Since 1865)*. New York: Knopf, 1959, p. 147.

30. Billington, *Westward to the Pacific*, p. 101.

31. Frederick Jackson Turner, "The Significance of the Frontier in American History," American Historical Association, *Annual Report for 1893*. Washington, DC: Government Printing Office, 1894, p. 3.

32. White, *"It's Your Misfortune and None of My Own,"* p. 58.

# 1

# THE LURE
# OF THE WEST

# CHAPTER PREFACE

For the first few decades after the original thirteen colonies won their independence from Great Britain, westward expansion occurred east of the Mississippi as farmers settled fertile but untamed areas in Kentucky, Tennessee, Ohio, Indiana, Illinois, Michigan, and other regions. The Spanish and others had explored and partially settled some of the West Coast, but during the eighteenth century little was known about the vast area west of the Mississippi and east of the Stony Mountains (as the Rockies were called at the time of the Revolution).

Westward expansion began in earnest with the Louisiana Purchase. In 1801 France claimed ownership of the Louisiana Territory, which was defined as the area between the Mississippi and the Rocky Mountains, north of Texas, and south of the Columbia River—roughly the middle third of the modern United States. However, in that year France, in secret negotiations, agreed to sell the Louisiana Territory to the United States for $15 million, to help finance Napoléon Bonaparte's military campaign in Europe. The Louisiana Purchase doubled the size of the nation, and in 1803 President Thomas Jefferson commissioned the Lewis and Clark expedition to explore the new territory.

Lewis and Clark's return to the East in 1806 greatly stimulated interest in the West. Lewis and Clark's reports of beavers and other animals valued for their hides made the Rocky Mountain fur trade a lucrative enterprise during the 1820s. During the 1830s and 1840s, the explorers' description of the Pacific Northwest encouraged thousands of settlers to make the transcontinental journey west along the Oregon Trail.

After Lewis and Clark, the next great event to draw settlers west was the California gold rush. After gold was discovered in 1848 at Sutter's Mill, near what is now Sacramento, California, thousands of "49ers" rushed to California the following year. Most came hoping to strike it rich and then return home, but many stayed in their new homes, finding work as farmers or merchants rather than as miners. Other gold and silver rushes happened throughout the nineteenth century in Colorado, Nevada, Alaska, and other states. In each case the mineral strike contributed greatly to the state's economic development.

Whether they hoped to become traders, farmers, miners, or something else, the pioneers who drove America's westward expansion had one thing in common: They were seeking a better life for themselves and their families. As westward expansion ran its course throughout the nineteenth century, the seemingly unlimited amounts of unclaimed land and natural resources to be found on the western frontier earned America its reputation as a land of opportunity.

# To Find a Northwest Passage

*Thomas Jefferson*

When Thomas Jefferson became president in 1801, the western two-thirds of North America was largely unmapped, and few Americans thought that their nation could govern an area so vast. Jefferson, however, envisioned the United States as an "Empire of Liberty" that would one day reach the Pacific. To further the course of westward expansion, Jefferson appointed army captain Meriwether Lewis and his friend William Clark to lead a transcontinental expedition.

Lewis and Clark's mission was to find a Northwest Passage—an all-water route to the Pacific—which Jefferson hoped would lead to rich trade with the Orient. Although they found no such route, their two-and-a-half-year journey vastly increased the fledgling nation's knowledge of what lay west of the Mississippi. In this June 20, 1803, letter to Lewis, Jefferson outlines the purpose and functions of the expedition.

As you read, consider the following questions:
1. What kinds of knowledge about the West did Jefferson hope to obtain through the expedition?
2. What were Jefferson's greatest concerns about the expedition?
3. How does Jefferson instruct Lewis and Clark to treat new Indian tribes they may encounter?

Excerpted from "Letter of Instruction to Lewis and Clark," by Thomas Jefferson, *The West in the History of the Nation: A Reader, Volume One: To 1877*, edited by William F. Deverell and Anne F. Hyde (Boston: St. Martin's Press, 2000).

*To Meriwether Lewis, esquire, Captain of the 1st regiment of infantry of the United States of America:* Your situation as Secretary of the President of the United States has made you acquainted with the objects of my confidential message of Jan. 18, 1803, to the legislature. you have seen the act they passed, which, tho' expressed in general terms, was meant to sanction those objects, and you are appointed to carry them into execution.

Instruments for ascertaining by celestial observations the geography of the country thro' which you will pass, have already been provided. light articles for barter, & presents among the Indians, arms for your attendants, say for from 10 to 12 men, boats, tents, & other travelling apparatus, with ammunition, medicine, surgical instruments & provisions you will have prepared with such aids as the Secretary at War can yield in his department. . . .

Your mission has been communicated to the Ministers here from France, Spain & Great Britain, and through them to their governments: and such assurances given them as to it's objects as we trust will satisfy them. the country of Louisiana [roughly defined as the area between the Mississippi and the Rocky Mountains] having been ceded by Spain to France, the passport you have from the Minister of France, the representative of the present sovereign of the country, will be a protection with all it's subjects: And that from the Minister of England will entitle you to the friendly aid of any traders of that allegiance with whom you may happen to meet.

## The Northwest Passage

The object of your mission is to explore the Missouri river, & such principal stream of it, as, by it's course & communication with the waters of the Pacific Ocean, may offer the most direct & practicable water communication across this continent, for the purposes of commerce.

Beginning at the mouth of the Missouri, you will take observations of latitude & longitude, at all remarkable points on the river, & especially at the mouths of rivers, at rapids, at islands & other places & objects distinguished by such natural marks & characters of a durable kind, as that they may with certainty be recognized hereafter. the courses of the river between these points of observation may be supplied by the compass, the log-line & by time, corrected by the observations themselves. the variations of the compass too, in different places, should be noticed.

The interesting points of portage between the heads of the Missouri & the water offering the best communication with the Pacific Ocean should also be fixed by observation, & the course of that water to the ocean, in the same manner as that of the Missouri.

Your observations are to be taken with great pains & accuracy, to be entered distinctly, & intelligibly for others as well as yourself, to comprehend all the elements necessary, with the aid of the usual tables, to fix the latitude and longitude of the places at which they were taken, & are to be rendered to the war office, for the purpose of having the calculations made concurrently by proper persons within the U.S. . . . .

## Gathering Knowledge

The commerce which may be carried on with the people inhabiting the line you will pursue, renders a knolege of these people important. you will therefore endeavor to make yourself acquainted, as far as a diligent pursuit of your journey shall admit,

their relations with other tribes or nations;
their language, traditions, monuments;
their ordinary occupations in agriculture, fishing, hunting, war, arts, & the implements for these;
their food, clothing, & domestic accomodations;
the diseases prevalent among them, & the remedies they use; moral & physical circumstances which distinguish them from the tribes we know;
peculiarities in their laws, customs & dispositions;
and articles of commerce they may need or furnish, & to what extent.

And considering the interest which every nation has in extending & strengthening the authority of reason & justice among the people around them, it will be useful to acquire what knolege you can of the state of morality, religion & information among them, as it may better enable those who endeavor to civilize & instruct them, to adapt their measures to the existing notions & practises of those on whom they are to operate.

Other object worthy of notice will be

the soil & face of the country, it's growth & vegetable productions; especially those not of the U.S.

the animals of the country generally, & especially those not known in the U.S.

the remains and accounts of any which may deemed rare or extinct;

the mineral productions of every kind; but more particularly metals, limestone, pit coal & salpetre; salines & mineral waters, noting the temperature of the last, & such circumstances as may indicate their character.

Volcanic appearances.

climate as characterized by the thermometer, by the proportion of rainy, cloudy & clear days, by lightening, hail, snow, ice, by the access & recess of frost, by the winds prevailing at different seasons, the dates at which particular plants put forth or lose their flowers, or leaf, times of appearance of particular birds, reptiles or insects.

Altho' your route will be along the channel of the Missouri, yet you will endeavor to inform yourself, by inquiry, of the character & extent of the country watered by it's branches, & especially on it's southern side. the North river or Rio Bravo [the Rio Grande] which runs into the gulph of Mexico, and the North river, or Rio colorado, which runs into the gulph of California, are understood to be the principal streams heading opposite to the waters of the Missouri, and running Southwardly. whether the dividing grounds between the Missouri & them are mountains or flatlands, what are their distance from the Missouri, the character of the intermediate country, & the people inhabiting it, are worthy of particular enquiry. The Northern waters of the Missouri are less to be enquired after, because they have been ascertained to a considerable degree, and are still in a course of ascertainment by English traders & travellers. but if you can learn anything certain of the most Northern source of the Missisipi, & of it's position relative to the lake of the woods [a lake on the Canada-Minnesota border], it will be interesting to us. some account too of the path of the Canadian traders from the Missisipi, at the mouth of the Ouisconsin [Wisconsin] river, to where it strikes the Missouri and of the soil & rivers in it's course, is desireable.

## Encounters with the Natives
In all your intercourse with the natives treat them in the most friendly & conciliatory manner which their own conduct will admit; allay all jealousies as to the object of your journey, satisfy them of it's innocence, make them acquainted with the position, extent, character, peaceable & commercial dispositions of the U.S. of our wish to be neighborly, friendly & useful to them, & of our dispositions to a commercial intercourse with them; confer with them on the points most convenient as mutual emporiums [trading houses], & the articles of most desireable interchange for them & us. if a few of their influential chiefs, within practicable distance, wish to visit us, arrange such a visit with them, and furnish them with authority to call on our officers, on their entering the U.S. to have them conveyed to this place at public expence. if any of them should wish to have some of their young people brought up with us, & taught such arts as may be useful to them, we will receive, instruct & take care of them. such a mission, whether of influential chiefs, or of young people, would give some security to your own party. carry with you some matter of the kine-pox [a serum used as a vaccine against

smallpox], inform those of them with whom you may be of it's efficacy as a preservative from the small-pox; and instruct & incourage them in the use of it. this may be especially done wherever you winter.

As it is impossible for us to foresee in what manner you will be recieved by those people, whether with hospitality or hostility, so is it impossible to prescribe the exact degree of perseverance with which you are to pursue your journey. we value too much the lives of citizens to offer them to probably destruction. your numbers will be sufficient to secure you against the unauthorised opposition of individuals, or of small parties: but if a superior force, authorised or not authorised, by a nation, should be arrayed against your further passage, & inflexibly determined to arrest it, you must decline it's further pursuit, and return. in the loss of yourselves, we should lose also the information you will have acquired. by returning safely with that, you may enable us to renew the essay with better calculated means. to your own discretion therefore must be left the degree of danger you may risk, & the point at which you should decline, only saying we wish you to err on the side of your safety, & bring back your party safe, even if it be with less information. . . .

Should you reach the Pacific ocean inform yourself of the circumstances which may decide whether the furs of those parts may not be collected as advantageously at the head of the Missouri (convenient as is supposed to the waters of the Colorado & Oregon or Columbia) as at Nootka sound [a bay on the coast of British Columbia] or any other point of that coast; & that trade be consequently conducted through the Missouri & U.S. more beneficially than by the circumnavigation now practised.

## Returning Home

On your arrival on that coast endeavor to learn if there be any port within your reach frequented by the sea-vessels of any nation, and to send two of your trusty people back by sea, in such way as shall appear practicable, with a copy of your notes. and should you be of opinion that the return of your party by the way they went will be eminently dangerous, then ship the whole, & return by sea by way of Cape Horn or the Cape of good Hope, as you shall be able. . . .

Should you find it safe to return by the way you go, after sending two of your party round by sea, or with your whole party, if no conveyance by sea can be found, do so; making such observations on your return as may serve to supply, correct or confirm those made on your outward journey.

In re-entering the U.S. and reaching a place of safety, discharge any of your attendants who may desire & deserve it, procuring for them immediate paiment of all arrears of pay & cloathing which may have incurred since their departure; & assure them that they shall be recommended to the liberality of the legislature for the grant of a soldier's portion of land each, as proposed in my message to Congress & repair yourself with your papers to the seat of government. . . .

Given under my hand at the city of Washington, this 20th day of June 1803

Th. Jefferson
Pr. US. of America

# The Advantages of Settling the Pacific Northwest

*Hall J. Kelley*

A major phase of westward expansion began in the 1840s when "Oregon fever" gripped America and thousands of settlers set out for the Oregon Territory. Many of these pioneers were inspired by Boston schoolteacher Hall J. Kelley—the so-called "Prophet of Oregon"—who had been captivated with the Pacific Northwest ever since reading the Lewis and Clark journals as a child. In 1829 Kelley founded the American Society for Encouraging Settlement of the Oregon Territory, which published "A Geographical Sketch of That Part of North America Called Oregon" the following year. The promotional pamphlet, excerpted below, describes the benefits of settling in the Oregon Territory and urges the U.S. government to take permanent possession of it from the British, who had a partial claim to the region.

As you read, consider the following questions:
1. What does Kelley fear will happen if Americans do not settle Oregon?
2. According to the author, what industries are most profitable in Oregon?
3. How does Kelley view the Indian tribes of Oregon?

---

The local position of that country; its physical appearance and productions; its qualities of soil and climate, suggest,

Excerpted from *A Geographical Sketch of That Part of North America Called Oregon*, by Hall J. Kelley (Hall J. Kelley, 1830).

not only the practicability of founding a colony in it; but the consequent beneficial results to our Republic; and the many valuable blessings it might be made to yield to the settlers, and to their posterity. . . . It is the object of these remarks to notice some of the advantages, which would inevitably accrue to the government of the United States, from a colonization of that country.

*First*. The occupancy of it, by three thousand of the active sons of American freedom, would secure it from the possession of another nation, and from augmenting the power and physical resources of an enemy. It might save that and this country, from the disastrous consequences of a foreign and corrupt population; and benefit mankind by a race of people, whose past lives, affording the most honourable testimony of their characters, would be a pledge for their future conduct, and a full indemnity for all expenses incurred in their behalf.

It is not doubtful hypothesis, that unless our legitimate rights on the waters and in the territory of Oregon, are protected by planting a colony in it, or by other means no less effectual; they will in a few years more, become entirely lost to our merchants, or to the benefits of our country. . . .

*Second*. A free and exclusive trade with the Indians, and with a colony in Oregon, would very considerably increase the resources, and promote the commercial and manufacturing interests of our country.

The fur trade has been and still is found, vastly lucrative to those who pursue it. The contemplated colony would find it productive of great pecuniary advantage. . . . The traffic carried on with the Indians will become more reciprocal, and equal in the diffusion of its comforts, as industry and the peaceful arts are sustained by them; for a trade with any people is commensurate with their real wants; these, with Indians, must naturally increase, as they assimilate their customs and habits to those of their refined and civilized neighbours. . . .

English traders . . . have conciliated the friendship of the natives, and secured a profitable trade with them, which consists chiefly in beads and many other articles of no value. . . . The exclusive privilege, therefore, of supplying these articles, would be alike beneficial to the [American] merchant and the manufacturer, and would contribute to the wealth and prosperity of the country. . . .

*Third.* The fisheries might be more extensively and profitably pursued. They have long constituted a valuable branch of our commerce, and a perennial and vital source of our comforts and prosperity. . . .

*Fourth.* A port of entry, and a naval station at the mouth of the Columbia, or in De Fuca straits, would be of immense importance to a protection of the whale and other fisheries, and of the fur trade; and to a general control over the Pacific ocean. . . . The great abundance of excellent timber of ship building; and the small comparative expense, at which ships of war might be built on the banks of the Columbia, would justify the making of navy yards, and building, in them, the principal part of our public and private vessels. . . .

*Fifth.* It is an object, worthy the attention of government, to secure the friendship of the Indians, and prevent alliances between them and other nations.

By cultivating a friendly intercourse, and coalition with them, they might not only be prevented from cooperating with an enemy; but if desirable, be induced to oppose his attacks. . . .

The American government ought to hold no sovereignty over the Indians without doing them good, and in order to bless and be blessed, it is not enough simply to occupy their territory. The settlers must consider them in the relation of children, and treat them with the tender solicitude and kindness of parents. . . . Let them be directed and assisted in cultivating, at first, small parcels of fertile ground; and let them receive the entire products. Let them, furthermore, share variously in the benefits of society;—their children be educated in the common schools of the Colony, and they will be made happy and useful. . . .

*Sixth.* The settlement of the Oregon country, would conduce to a freer intercourse, and a more extensive and lucrative trade with the East Indies.

Commerce would break away from its present narrow and prescribed limits, and spread into new and broader channels, embracing within its scope, China, Corea, the Phillipine and Spice islands, Japan and its provinces. . . . The colony located on a shore of easy access; and measuring its conduct by a policy, liberal and universal, will find no difficulties in opening with that civilized people, a free intercourse, and consequently, inexhaustible sources of wealth and prosperity. . . .

Such an extension and enjoyment of the East Indian trade, would provoke the spirit of American enterprize, to open communications from the Mississippi valley, and from the gulf of Mexico to the Pacific ocean, and thus open *new channels*, through which the products of America and the Eastern world, will pass in mutual exchange, saving in every voyage, a distance of ten thousand miles. . . .

*Seventh.* Many of our seaports would be considerably benefited by taking emigrants from their redundant population. . . . Multitudes of such persons, sustaining the character of worthy citizens, cast out of employment, into idleness and poverty, might wisely emigrate to a country, where they could pursue usely occupations, to which they are competent, with profit. . . .

The learned professions might spare some of their wise and erudite votaries who, in Oregon, could find meeds of immortal honours. . . .

These hastily written observations must be concluded by the remark, that all nations, who have planted colonies, have been enriched by them. . . . America has a better opportunity, and fairer prospects of success. . . . She can set up in business, her full grown and more affectionate children nearer home; and on a richer inheritance; and can receive to herself greater benefits. The present period is propitious to the experiment. The free governments of the world are fast progressing to the consummation of moral excellence; and are embracing within the scope of their policies, the benevolent and meliorating principles of humanity and reform. The most enlightened nation on earth will not be insensible to the best means of national prosperity. Convinced of the utility and happy consequences of establishing the Oregon colony, the American Republic will found, protect and cherish it; and thus enlarge the sphere of human felicity, and extend the peculiar blessings of civil polity, and of the Christian religion, to distant and destitute nations.

# Inciting Gold Fever

*James K. Polk*

Few events spurred development of the American West more than the discovery of gold in California. Within just eighteen months of the initial January 24, 1848, discovery, over forty thousand gold-seekers arrived at the California "diggings." Relatively few of them found wealth, but the gold rush nevertheless stimulated economic growth in California and throughout the nation.

News of the gold rush spread relatively slowly. Many of the first reports of the discovery were viewed with skepticism in the East. "Gold fever" only truly set in after President James K. Polk substantiated the rumors of California gold in his December 1848 State of the Union address to Congress, excerpted below. This official confirmation was enough to prompt thousands of "49ers" to head west in the following months.

As you read, consider the following questions:
1. How have the reports of gold in California been corroborated, according to President Polk?
2. How will the discovery of gold in California affect the value of the U.S. dollar in relation to European currencies, in the president's view?
3. Do you feel that Polk's remarks exaggerate the amount or importance of gold in California? Why or why not?

Upper California, irrespective of the vast mineral wealth recently developed there, holds at this day, in point of value and importance, to the rest of the Union the same relation that Louisiana did when that fine territory was acquired

Excerpted from James K. Polk's State of the Union Address, December 5, 1848.

from France forty-five years ago. Extending nearly ten degrees of latitude along the Pacific, and embracing the only safe and commodious harbors on that coast for many hundred miles, with a temperate climate and an extensive interior of fertile lands, it is scarcely possible to estimate its wealth until it shall be brought under the government of our laws and its resources fully developed. From its position it must command the rich commerce of China, of Asia, of the islands of the Pacific, of western Mexico, of Central America, the South American States, and of the Russian possessions bordering on that ocean. A great emporium will doubtless speedily arise on the Californian coast which may be destined to rival in importance New Orleans itself. The depot of the vast commerce which must exist on the Pacific will probably be at some point on the Bay of San Francisco, and will occupy the same relation to the whole western coast of that ocean as New Orleans does to the valley of the Mississippi and the Gulf of Mexico. To this depot our numerous whale ships will resort with their cargoes to trade, refit, and obtain supplies. This of itself will largely contribute to build up a city, which would soon become the center of a great and rapidly increasing commerce. Situated on a safe harbor, sufficiently capacious for all the navies as well as the marine of the world, and convenient to excellent timber for shipbuilding, owned by the United States, it must become our great Western naval depot.

## The Supply Is Very Large

It was known that mines of the precious metals existed to a considerable extent in California at the time of its acquisition. Recent discoveries render it probable that these mines are more extensive and valuable than was anticipated. The accounts of the abundance of gold in that territory are of such an extraordinary character as would scarcely command belief were they not corroborated by the authentic reports of officers in the public service who have visited the mineral district and derived the facts which they detail from personal observation. Reluctant to credit the reports in general circulation as to the quantity of gold, the officer commanding our forces in California visited the mineral district in July last for the purpose of obtaining accurate information on the subject. His report to the War Department of the result of his examination and the facts obtained on the spot is herewith laid before Congress. When he visited the country there were about 4,000 persons engaged in collecting gold. There is every reason to believe that the number of persons so employed has since been augmented. The explorations already made warrant the belief that the supply is very large and that gold is found at various places in an extensive district of country.

Information received from officers of the Navy and other sources, though not so full and minute, confirms the accounts of the commander of our military force in California. It appears also from these reports that mines of quicksilver are found in the vicinity of the gold region. One of them is now being worked, and is believed to be among the most productive in the world.

The effects produced by the discovery of these rich mineral deposits and the success which has attended the labors of those who have resorted to them have produced a surprising change in the state of affairs in California. Labor commands a most exorbitant price, and all other pursuits but that of searching for the precious metals are abandoned. Nearly the whole of the male population of the country have gone to the gold districts. Ships arriving on the coast are deserted by their crews and their voyages suspended for want of sailors. Our commanding officer there entertains apprehensions that soldiers can not be kept in the public service without a large increase of pay. Desertions in his command have become frequent, and he recommends that those who shall withstand the strong temptation and remain faithful should be rewarded.

This abundance of gold and the all-engrossing pursuit of it have already caused in California an unprecedented rise in the price of all the necessaries of life.

That we may the more speedily and fully avail ourselves

of the undeveloped wealth of these mines, it is deemed of vast importance that a branch of the Mint of the United States be authorized to be established at your present session in California. Among other signal advantages which would result from such an establishment would be that of raising the gold to its par value in that territory. A branch mint of the United States at the great commercial depot on the west coast would convert into our own coin not only the gold derived from our own rich mines, but also the bullion and specie which our commerce may bring from the whole west coast of Central and South America. The west coast of America and the adjacent interior embrace the richest and best mines of Mexico, New Granada, Central America, Chili, and Peru. The bullion and specie drawn from these countries, and especially from those of western Mexico and Peru, to an amount in value of many millions of dollars, are now annually diverted and carried by the ships of Great Britain to her own ports, to be recoined or used to sustain her national bank, and thus contribute to increase her ability to command so much of the commerce of the world. If a branch mint be established at the great commercial point upon that coast, a vast amount of bullion and specie would flow thither to be recoined, and pass thence to New Orleans, New York, and other Atlantic cities. The amount of our constitutional currency at home would be greatly increased, while its circulation abroad would be promoted. It is well known to our merchants trading to China and the west coast of America that great inconvenience and loss are experienced from the fact that our coins are not current at their par value in those countries.

## The Vast Importance and Commercial Advantages of California

The powers of Europe, far removed from the west coast of America by the Atlantic Ocean, which intervenes, and by a tedious and dangerous navigation around the southern cape of the continent of America, can never successfully compete with the United States in the rich and extensive commerce which is opened to us at so much less cost by the acquisition of California.

The vast importance and commercial advantages of California have heretofore remained undeveloped by the Government of the country of which it constituted a part. Now that this fine province is a part of our country, all the States of the Union, some more immediately and directly than others, are deeply interested in the speedy development of its wealth and resources. No section of our country is more interested or will be more benefited than the commercial, navigating, and manufacturing interests of the Eastern States. Our planting and farming interests in every part of the Union will be greatly benefited by it. As our commerce and navigation are enlarged and extended, our exports of agricultural products and of manufactures will be increased, and in the new markets thus opened they can not fail to command remunerating and profitable prices.

The acquisition of California and New Mexico, the settlement of the Oregon boundary, and the annexation of Texas, extending to the Rio Grande, are results which, combined, are of greater consequence and will add more to the strength and wealth of the nation than any which have preceded them since the adoption of the Constitution.

# "Boosters" Promote Westward Migration

*Ned E. Farrell*

A major impetus to westward expansion in the latter half of the nineteenth century was the propaganda put out by western merchants, landowners, and railroad companies, who had a financial interest in helping western towns to thrive. These "boosters" circulated pamphlets in the East encouraging western migration. One such pamphlet, touting the benefits of Colorado, is excerpted below. The 1868 tract romanticizes the frontier as a land of abundance, where hard work was rewarded and where able-bodied men and women could make new lives for themselves.

As you read, consider the following questions:
1. What types of work are available in Colorado, according to the author?
2. How does the author describe the risks involved in settling in Colorado?
3. Do you feel that this booster pamphlet is persuasive? Why or why not?

---

Those who can do well in the west, are the producing class, the farmer, stock-raiser, wool-grower, dairyman, miner, and laborer. The natural wealth is there, but a great drawback, common to all our mining countries, has been the want of a permanent class of settlers, who will go, prepared to stay and build up homes. All are fast finding out that the climate, resources and advantages, more than repay for the privations attendant on settling in a new country. Those

Excerpted from *Colorado, the Rocky Mountain Gem, as It Is in 1868*, by Ned E. Farrell (Chicago: Chicago Western News Company, 1868).

who wish to settle in a new country, and grow up with it, and have a location that is pleasant to live in, with good society and the comforts of a life in the east, can find it now among the towns of Colorado. Doctors are not in demand, the climate is too healthy; from its great elevation and distance from large bodies of water, it cannot be otherwise. Many who have left the east, despairing and hopeless, have soon recovered, and rejoiced in restored health, renewed energies and prospects. Politicians are plenty, as in all new countries, and of legal talent there is no lack; few states, old or new, can boast a better standard class of legislators or members of the bar.

School teachers are well paid, and good ones are always in demand, as the rising generation are increasing very rapidly, the country being exceedingly productive in young ideas to be taught how to shoot.

Servant girls get from $10 to $12 per week, and if steady and reliable, find good homes among the best families. These prices should, and probably will be reduced somewhat, but from the lightness of the air, dryness of the atmosphere, and various other causes, servant girls seem to get in the notion of setting up housekeeping, and thus vacancies are frequent, and often hard to fill. A thousand could probably now obtain good situations or husbands in Colorado.

Mining labor is always in demand, and at better prices, considering cost of living, than any other mining country so easily reached.

## The Rewards of Honest Labor

Fortune-hunters, who expect to get rich in a month, will likely be disappointed; if getting rich was so easy, there are sharp men there to take advantage of it. Whoever goes to Colorado or any other mining country, with an idea that gold digging is not labor, had better get that idea out of their heads at once, and those who expect to live without work, will find poor encouragement in that country.

Fast young men who are only useful in carrying a gold-headed cane, will not find it a paying business.

Rogues and light-fingered gentry do not thrive. They seem to become afflicted with a throat disease, caused by too close contact with a rope.

But there is a constant demand for honest labor, and those who have no capital but their muscle, cannot do better than in Colorado. If they do not get above their business when they arrive, they need not starve, as they are doing by thousands in our large cities and in Europe. Cooperative clubs might be formed in every settlement in the east, of 10 or 20 persons, assessing the members enough to pay the expenses of one or two of the party, who could go ahead and select a location for the balance. This would be a saving of time and expense on the part of many, who can ill afford to spend a hundred dollars and their time for the trip, but could work and help pay for some one else to go in their stead.

"Nothing ventured nothing gained." Thousands in our Eastern States, millions in Europe, would be glad to have a home in the west, if they only *knew* they would have no bad luck. Of course all cannot succeed in everything; some failures will occur, but those who are struggling for a mere living, and have families to feed, should seek the west, put all together they can, and move on before all the best chances are taken, somewhere, anywhere out of the crowded cities. The great west has a plenty, and room for all; the poorest may be a peer if the stuff is in him; as a boy once wrote from the west to his father in the east, "some very small men get elected to office here; you better come on."

Thousands are led to go to new countries, on account of stories of fabulous wealth just discovered, where all can get rich. Don't rush. Just reflect a little, and remember there are other men as smart as you already on the ground, and prepared to pick up all the big things. If you go west, prepared to work for what you get, go ahead. If you are doing well, stay at home, but if you are out of business, no opening offers, you are desperate, bound to go somewhere, or commit suicide, don't do it. Go west, by all means, and give your spirit vent; a live man in the west, is worth a half dozen dead ones anywhere.

# Letters to Europe Extol the Virtues of America's Frontier

*Part I: Gjert Gregoriussen; Part II: C.F. Carlsson*

For many immigrants, one of the main attractions of America was the widespread availability of land. In Europe, land ownership was restricted to the aristocracy, but in nineteenth-century America there were countless acres waiting to be settled. The lure of cheap land, coupled with the relative poverty of their home countries, drew many Scandinavian immigrants to the Midwest from the 1840s through the 1880s. Like other immigrant groups, they wrote home, reporting on their successes and failures. Success stories of early immigrants, such as the two excerpted below, encouraged others to immigrate to frontier America.

In the first letter, Norwegian farmer Gjert Gregoriussen praises the economic opportunities and political freedom to be found in America. In the second letter, Swedish immigrant C.F. Carlsson emphasizes the warm welcome he received from neighbors after settling in Nebraska.

As you read, consider the following questions:
1. What specific aspects of the American political system does the author of the first letter praise?
2. How does the author of the second letter describe the fortune that other immigrants have had in America?
3. How great an effect do you imagine these letters had on their recipients?

Part I: Excerpted from "A Typical American Letter," by Gjert Gregoriussen, *Mississippi Valley Historical Review*, June 1922. Part II: Excerpted from "Letter to Dalarna from C.F. Carlsson," by C.F. Carlsson, February 1880.

# I

I must take this opportunity to let you know that we are in the best of health, and that we—both my wife and I—find ourselves exceedingly satisfied. Our son attends the English school, and talks English as well as the native born. Nothing has made me more happy and contented than the fact that we left Norway and journeyed to this country. We have gained more since our arrival here than I did during all the time that I lived in Norway, and I have every prospect of earning a livelihood here for myself and my family—even if my family were larger—so long as God gives me good health.

Such excellent plans have been developed here that even though one be infirm, no one need suffer want. Competent men are elected whose duty it is to see that no needy persons, either in the cities or in the country, shall have to beg for their living. If a man dies and is survived by a widow and children who are unable to support themselves—as is so often the case—they have the privilege of petitioning these officials. To each one will then be given every year as much as is needed of clothes and food, and no discrimination will be shown between the native-born and those from foreign countries. These things I have learned through daily observation, and I do not believe there can be better laws and arrangements . . . in the whole world. I have talked with a sensible person who has traveled in many countries, who has lived here twenty-six years, and has a full knowledge of the matter; both of him and of other reliable persons I have made inquiries, for I wish to let everyone know the truth.

When assemblies are held to elect officials who are to serve the country, the vote of the common man carries just as much authority and influence as does that of the rich and powerful man. Neither in the matter of clothes nor in seats are distinctions to be observed, whether one be a farmer or a clerk. The freedom which one enjoys is just as good as that of the other. So long as he comports himself honestly he will be subjected to no interference. Everybody has the liberty to travel about in the country, wherever he wishes, without any passports or papers. Everyone is permitted to engage in whatever business he finds most desirable, in trade or commerce, by land or by water. But if anyone is found guilty of crime, he will be prosecuted and severely punished for it.

No duties are levied upon goods which are produced in the country and brought to the city by water or by land. In case of death, no registration is required; the survivor, after paying the debts, is free to dispose of the property for himself and his family just as he desires. . . . It would heartily please me if I could learn that every one of you who are in need and have little chance of gaining support for yourselves and your families would make up your mind to leave Norway and come to America, for, even if many more were to come, there would still be room here for all. For all those who are willing to work there is no lack of employment and business here. It is possible for all to live in comfort and without suffering want. I do not believe that any of those who suffer under the oppression of others and who must rear their children under straitened circumstances could do better than to help the latter to come to America. But alas, many persons, even though they want to come, lack the necessary means and many others are so stupid as to believe that it is best to live in the country where they have been brought up even if they have nothing but hard bread to satisfy their hunger. It is as if they should say that those who move to a better land, where there is plenty, commit a wrong. But I can find no place where our Creator has forbidden one to seek one's food in an honorable manner. I should like to talk to many persons in Norway for a little while, but we do not wish to live in Norway. We lived there altogether too long. Nor have I talked with any immigrant in this country who wished to return.

# II

Much I have seen, heard, and experienced, but nothing unhappy, no shady sides. To be sure I believed when I departed from home, from the fatherland, from family, friends, and acquaintances, that everything would at first be rather unfamiliar. But no, strangely enough, everything is as I wished it should be. The country is beautiful, if any land on earth deserves to be called so. And if you compare conditions here with Sweden's, there is no similarity at all. The soil consists of a kind of dark loam over a layer of marl on a clay base; your finest plowlands at home cannot compare with the rich prairies here, where golden harvests grow from year to year without having to be manured or ditched. No stones, no stumps hinder the cultivator's plow. If you add to this that one can almost get such land as a gift or for an insignificant sum compared with its natural value, you soon have an idea why America is truly and undeniably better than old Sweden. But here is another thing, taxes do not consume the American farmer, they are extremely light. America maintains no expensive royal house, no inactive armies, which undermine the people's welfare; such things are considered here as superfluous articles and extremely harmful. Never has a freer people trodden, cultivated, and tended a better land than this. Hundreds of thousands of persons have found here the happiness they vainly sought in Europe's lands.

The greater part have come here without means, many even with debts. But with good will and an unshakable will to work they have within a few years gradually attained sustenance, prosperity, indeed quite often wealth. And still there is land for a hundred million people, as fabulous as this may sound. In twelve years the population of Nebraska has increased from thirty thousand to four hundred thousand; no other place in America can show such rapid growth. Swedes number around fifteen thousand in Nebraska. All are getting along well, and when you are getting along well you are not likely to long for what was not pleasant; even homesickness is fully cured. And as far as food is concerned, there is such great abundance here that one would be amazed, even if he were the greatest gourmet. To list everything here would surely be too long; let me therefore say that it is unfamiliar to us Swedes. Now someone may perhaps believe that there are bad persons and dangerous beasts here, but there is neither. When we arrived we heard from everyone's lips, welcome, heartily welcome, and they showed by their actions that they meant what they said; they invited us to eat as though we had been their nearest relatives. My traveling companion has bought eighty acres or tunnland of land for around fifty dollars. The climate is remarkably fine; nothing stands in our way except the language. We cannot understand their speech, but it is possible for us to learn as well as others have done. I see after this first short time that it is going well. And therefore you can understand that I do not regret the journey, other than to regret that I had not made it before. But better late than never, as the saying goes, and I agree.

There is no forest here in Nebraska to speak of, but there is so much corn that it is used for fuel instead of firewood. Corn is also given to the large pigs which are raised for sale. Rivers flow through the land in all directions, railroads also cross it in all directions.

I have recently finished with my job; I also worked for a railroad company, where at first we got one and a quarter, but at the end one and a half dollars, and we paid three and a half dollars per man a week for room and board. But a family can live on three dollars a week, no matter how large the family may be. We had to quit our job because the ground froze, but we will begin again at the end of February when the weather turns milder. They start sowing and driving out onto the fields at the end of February and the beginning of March. I am doing fine and I expect to do better when I can learn the language. I shall now go to school and learn English for five or six weeks, which anyone can do gratis.

# Free Land in Oklahoma

Harper's Weekly

By the 1880s the western plains were being settled more rapidly than ever before. In 1862 the government had passed the Homestead Act, which promised free plots to settlers willing to farm the land for five years. By the 1880s, however, these free lands were running out. In response to pressure from would-be homesteaders, in 1889 the U.S. government opened 2 million acres of modern-day Oklahoma—which had previously been promised to several Indian tribes—to white settlement. The lands were officially opened to homesteaders at noon on April 22, 1889. Thousands of settlers lined up along the borders of the district, waiting for the bugles that marked the start of the race for land. In the following *Harper's Weekly* report on the event, a correspondent details the chaos and corruption that characterized the Oklahoma land rush.

As you read, consider the following questions:
1. Do you think that the author's account of the race is overly dramatized, or has he effectively captured the tense atmosphere of the event?
2. What is the author's opinion of those who cheated by staking out plots of land before the appointed hour?
3. To what does the author attribute the remarkably low levels of violence that followed the rush for free land?

---

The preparations for the settlement of Oklahoma had been complete, even to the slightest detail, for weeks before the opening day. The Santa Fe Railway, which runs through Oklahoma north and south, was prepared to take any

Excerpted from "The Rush to Oklahoma," *Harper's Weekly*, May 18, 1889.

number of people from its handsome station at Arkansas City, Kansas, and to deposit them in almost any part of Oklahoma as soon as the law allowed; thousands of covered wagons were gathered in camps on all sides of the new Territory waiting for the embargo to be lifted. In its picturesque aspects the rush across the border at noon on the opening day must go down in history as one of the most noteworthy events of Western civilization. At the time fixed, thousands of hungry home-seekers, who had gathered from all parts of the country, and particularly from Kansas and Missouri, were arranged in line along the border, ready to lash their horses into furious speed in the race for fertile spots in the beautiful land before them. The day was one of perfect peace. Overhead the sun shone down from a sky as fair and blue as the cloudless heights of Colorado. The whole expanse of space from zenith to horizon was spotless in its blue purity. The clear spring air, through which the rolling green billows of the promised land could be seen with unusual distinctness for many miles, was as sweet and fresh as the balmy atmosphere of June among New Hampshire's hills.

## Rampant Cheating

As the expectant home-seekers waited with restless patience, the clear, sweet notes of a cavalry bugle rose and hung a moment upon the startled air. It was noon. The last barrier of savagery in the United States was broken down. Moved by the same impulse, each driver lashed his horses furiously; each rider dug his spurs into his willing steed, and each man on foot caught his breath hard and darted forward. A cloud of dust rose where the home-seekers had stood in line, and when it had drifted away before the gentle breeze, the horses and wagons and men were tearing across the open country like fiends. The horsemen had the best of it from the start. It was a fine race for a few minutes, but soon the riders began to spread out like a fan, and by the time they had reached the horizon they were scattered about as far as the eye could see. Even the fleetest of the horsemen found upon reaching their chosen localities that men in wagons and men on foot were there before them. As it was clearly impossible for a man on foot to out-run a horseman, the inference is plain that Oklahoma had been entered hours before the appointed time. Notwith-standing the assertions of the soldiers that every boomer had been driven out of Oklahoma, the fact remains that the woods along the various streams within Oklahoma were literally full of people Sunday night. Nine-tenths of these people made settlement upon the land illegally. The other tenth would have done so had there been any desirable land left to settle upon. This action on the part of the first claimholders will cause a great deal of land litigation in the future, as it is not to be expected that the man who ran his horse at its utmost speed for ten miles only to find a settler with an ox team in quiet possession of his chosen farm will tamely submit to this plain infringement of the law.

Some of the men who started from the line on foot were quite as successful in securing desirable claims as many who rode fleet horses. They had the advantage of knowing just where their land was located. One man left the line with the others, carrying on his back a tent, a blanket, some camp dishes, an axe, and provisions for two days. He ran down the railway track for six miles, and reached his claim in just sixty minutes. Upon arriving on his land he fell down under a tree, unable to speak or see. I am glad to be able to say that his claim is one of the best in Oklahoma. The rush from the line was so impetuous that by the time the first railway train arrived from the north at twenty-five minutes past twelve o'clock, only a few of the hundreds of boomers were anywhere to be seen. The journey of this first train was well-nigh as interesting as the rush of the men in wagons. The train left Arkansas City at 8.45 o'clock in the forenoon. It consisted of an empty baggage car, which was set apart for the use of the newspaper corre-spondents, eight passenger coaches, and the caboose of a freight train. The coaches were so densely packed with men that not another human being could get on board. So uncomfortably crowded were they that some of the younger boomers climbed to the roofs of the cars and clung perilously to the ventilators. An adventurous person secured at great risk a seat on the forward truck of the baggage car.

## High Hopes and Deep Disappointment

In this way the train was loaded to its utmost capacity. That no one was killed or injured was due as much to the careful management of the train as to the ability of the passengers to take care of themselves. Like their friends in the wagons, the boomers on the cars were exultant with joy at the thought of at last entering into possession of the promised land. At first appearances the land through which the train ran seemed to justify all the virtues that had been claimed for it. The rolling, grassy uplands, and the wooded river-bottoms, the trees in which were just bursting into the most beautiful foliage of early spring, seemed to give a close reality to the distant charm of green and purple forest growths, which rose from the trough of some long swell and went heaving away to meet the brighter hues in the far-off sky. Throughout all the landscape were clumps of trees suggesting apple orchards set in fertile meadows, and here and there were dim patches of gray and white sand that might in a less barbarous region be mistaken for farm-houses surrounded by hedges and green fields. Truly the Indians have well-named Oklahoma the "beautiful land." The landless and home-hungry people on the train might be pardoned their mental exhilaration, when the effect of this wonderfully beautiful country upon the most prosaic mind is fully considered. It was an eager and an exuberantly joyful crowd that rode slowly into Guthrie at twenty minutes past one o'clock on that perfect April afternoon. Men who had expected to lay out the town site were grievously disappointed at the first glimpse of their proposed scene of operations. The slope east of the railway at Guthrie station was dotted white with tents and sprinkled thick with men running about in all directions.

"We're done for," said a town-site speculator, in dismay.

"Some one has gone in ahead of us and laid out the town."

"Never mind that," shouted another townsite speculator, "but make a rush and get what you can."

Hardly had the train slackened its speed when the impatient boomers began to leap from the cars and run up the slope. Men jumped from the roofs of the moving cars at the risk of their lives. Some were so stunned by the fall that they could not get up for some minutes. The coaches were so crowded that many men were compelled to squeeze through the windows in order to get a fair start at the head of the crowd. Almost before the train had come to a standstill the cars were emptied. In their haste and eagerness, men fell over each other in heaps, others stumbled and fell headlong, while many ran forward so blindly and impetuously that it was not until they had passed the best of the town lots that they came to a realization of their actions.

## Abuse of Authority

I ran with the first of the crowd to get a good point of view from which to see the rush. When I had time to look about me I found that I was standing beside a tent, near which a man was leisurely chopping holes in the sod with a new axe.

"Where did you come from, that you have already pitched your tent?" I asked.

"Oh, I was here," said he.

"How was that?"

"Why, I was a deputy United States marshal."

"Did you resign?"

"No; I'm a deputy still."

"But it is not legal for a deputy United States marshal, or any one in the employ of the government, to take up a town lot in this manner."

"That may all be, stranger; but I've got two lots here, just the same; and about fifty other deputies have got lots in the same way. In fact, the deputy-marshals laid out the town."

At intervals of fifteen minutes, other trains came from the north loaded down with home-seekers and town-site speculators. As each succeeding crowd rushed up the slope and found that government officers had taken possession of the best part of the town, indignation became hot and outspoken; yet the marshals held to their lots and refused to move. Bloodshed was prevented only by the belief of the homeseekers that the government would set the matter right.

This course of the deputy United States marshals was one of the most outrageous pieces of imposition upon honest home-seekers ever practised in the settlement of a new country. That fifty men could, through influence, get themselves appointed as deputy United States marshals for the sole purpose of taking advantage of their positions in this way is creditable neither to them nor to the man who made their appointment possible. This illegal seizure thus became the first matter of public discussion in the city of Guthrie.

When the passengers from the first train reached the spot where the deputy-marshals had ceased laying out lots, they seized the line of the embryo street and ran it eastward as far as their numbers would permit. The second train load of people took it where the first let off, and ran it entirely out of sight behind a swell of ground at least two miles from the station. The following car loads of home-seekers went north and south, so that by the time that all were in for the day a city large enough in area to hold 100,000 inhabitants had been staked off, with more or less geometrical accuracy. A few women and children were in the rush, but they had to take their chances with the rest. Disputes over the ownership of lots grew incessant, for the reason that when a man went to the river for a drink of water, or tried to get his baggage at the railway station, another man would take possession of his lot, notwithstanding the obvious presence of the first man's stakes and sometimes part of his wearing apparel. Owing to the uncertainty concerning the lines of the streets, two and sometimes more lots were staked out on the same ground, each claimant hoping that the official survey would give him the preference. Contrary to all expectations, there was no bloodshed over the disputed lots. This may be accounted for by the fact that no intoxicating liquors of any kind were allowed to be sold in Oklahoma. It is a matter of common comment among the people that the peaceful way in which Oklahoma was settled was due entirely to its compulsory prohibition. Had whiskey been plentiful in Guthrie the disputed lots might have been watered in blood, for every man went armed with some sort of deadly weapon. If there could be a more striking temperance lesson than this, I certainly should like to see it.

When Congress gives Oklahoma some sort of government the prohibition of the sale of intoxicating liquor should be the first and foremost of her laws.

It is estimated that between six and seven thousand persons reached Guthrie by train from the north the first afternoon, and that fully three thousand came in by wagon from the north and east, and by train from Purcell on the south, thus making a total population for the first day of about ten thousand. By taking thought in the matter, three-fourths of these people had provided themselves with tents and blankets, so that even on the first night they had ample shelter from the weather. The rest of them slept the first night as best they could, with only the red earth for a pillow and the starry arch of heaven for a blanket. At dawn of Tuesday the unrefreshed home-seekers and town-site speculators arose, and began anew the location of disputed claims. The tents multiplied like mushrooms in a rain that day, and by night the building of frame houses had been begun in earnest in the new streets. The buildings were by no means elaborate, yet they were as good as the average frontier structure, and they served their purpose, which was all that was required.

On that day the trains going north were filled with returning boomers, disgusted beyond expression with the dismal outlook of the new country. Their places were taken by others who came in to see the fun, and perhaps pick up a bargain in the way of town lots or commercial speculation.

# 2

# CONQUEST OF NATIVE AMERICA

# CHAPTER PREFACE

Thomas Jefferson, the third president of the United States, was an enthusiastic supporter of American territorial expansion, but he was also concerned about how the westward movement would affect American Indians. Jefferson hoped that over time Native Americans would become "civilized" and assimilated into white culture. However, he also proposed a secondary solution. If certain tribes wanted to maintain their own lands and "savage" culture, he reasoned, they should move farther west, beyond the Mississippi River, where few whites had settled. In 1830 Indian removal became official U.S. policy with the passage of the Indian Removal Act. This law gave then-president Andrew Jackson the power to negotiate with tribes east of the Mississippi and to remove them to the West. Some tribes moved voluntarily; others were forced west by U.S. troops.

Tribes that moved west voluntarily did so based on the U.S. government's assurances that the Indian Territory would be theirs forever. This territory was originally defined, somewhat vaguely, as all U.S. territory west of the Mississippi. As westward expansion gained momentum, however, especially during the three decades following the Civil War, the Indian Territory was gradually restricted to present-day Oklahoma. In 1889 even this last vestige of the Indian Territory was opened to white settlers.

Many tribes resisted white encroachment on their lands, and the result was the North American Indian Wars. The period between 1860 and 1898 witnessed more violence between Indians and whites than ever before—938 skirmishes and battles, according to historian Gerald F. Kreyche. Among the most well-known incidents were the Sand Creek Massacre, in which U.S. troops killed hundreds of mostly unarmed Cheyenne and Arapaho, and the Battle of Little Big Horn, in which several tribes of Plains Indians scored their greatest victory against General George Armstrong Custer.

In the nineteenth century, Indian removal and the North American Indian Wars were some of the most controversial issues surrounding westward expansion. Critics condemned the army's brutal treatment of the Indians, but many western settlers lived in fear of Indian raids. The Indians had their own view of events, but it was often ignored.

# Indian Removal Will Benefit Both the Indians and the United States

*Andrew Jackson*

Andrew Jackson, who grew up in frontier Tennessee, was the first westerner to be elected president. In his 1829 message to Congress, excerpted below, Jackson discusses a growing controversy between the state of Georgia and the Cherokee Nation. Cherokee leaders had argued that under the principles of tribal sovereignty, Georgia had no claim to Cherokee lands that were within Georgia's borders. Jackson dismisses this claim, and instead proposes that the Cherokee, and indeed all tribes east of the Mississippi, move to lands west of the Mississippi. Jackson promises that an Indian Territory will be created there, into which white settlers will not be allowed to encroach.

Jackson framed his removal policy as being for the benefit of the Indians, and he originally proposed that Indian emigration to the West be voluntary. Throughout the 1830s, however, the U.S. Army forced tribes that resisted removal to emigrate to the western plains. In the most famous example, the U.S. Army removed the Cherokee from Georgia in a forced march to the Indian Territory. Thousands died along what became known as the Trail of Tears.

As you read, consider the following questions:
1. What objections does Jackson offer to the Cherokee's claim that theirs is a nation separate from the United States?

Excerpted from Andrew Jackson's First Annual Message to the United States Congress, December 8, 1829.

2. What fate does Jackson say awaits the Cherokee if they remain in Georgia?
3. What benefits does Jackson say that tribes will enjoy in the proposed Indian Territory?

---

The condition and ulterior destiny of the Indian tribes within the limits of some of our States have become objects of much interest and importance. It has long been the policy of Government to introduce among them the arts of civilization, in the hope of gradually reclaiming them from a wandering life. This policy has, however, been coupled with another wholly incompatible with its success. Professing a desire to civilize and settle them, we have at the same time lost no opportunity to purchase their lands and thrust them farther into the wilderness. By this means they have not only been kept in a wandering state, but been led to look upon us as unjust and indifferent to their fate. Thus, though lavish in its expenditures upon the subject, Government has constantly defeated its own policy, and the Indians in general, receding farther and farther to the west, have retained their savage habits. A portion, however, of the Southern tribes, having mingled much with the whites and made some progress in the arts of civilized life, have lately attempted to erect an independent government within the limits of Georgia and Alabama. These States, claiming to be the only sovereigns within their territories, extended their laws over the Indians, which induced the latter to call upon the United States for protection.

Under these circumstances the question presented was whether the General Government had a right to sustain these people in their pretensions. . . . If the General Government is not permitted to tolerate the erection of a confederate State within the territory of one of the members of this Union against her consent, much less could it allow a foreign and independent government to establish itself there. Georgia became a member of the Confederacy which eventuated in our Federal Union as a sovereign State. . . .

Alabama was admitted into the Union on the same footing with the original States. . . . There is no constitutional, conventional, or legal provision which allows them less power over the Indians within their borders than is possessed by Maine or New York. . . .

Actuated by this view of the subject, I informed the Indians inhabiting parts of Georgia and Alabama that their attempt to establish an independent government would not be countenanced by the Executive of the United States, and advised them to emigrate beyond the Mississippi or submit to the laws of those States.

## "To Preserve This Much-Injured Race"

Our conduct toward these people is deeply interesting to our national character. . . . By persuasion and force they have been made to retire from river to river and from mountain to mountain, until some of the tribes have become extinct and others have left but remnants to preserve for awhile their once terrible names. Surrounded by the whites with their arts of civilization, which by destroying the resources of the savage doom him to weakness and decay, the fate of the Mohegan, the Narragansett, and the Delaware is fast overtaking the Choctaw, the Cherokee, and the Creek. That this fate surely awaits them if they remain within the limits of the States does not admit of a doubt. Humanity and national honor demand that every effort should be made to avert so great a calamity. It is too late to inquire whether it was just in the United States to include them and their territory within the bounds of new States, whose limits they could control. That step can not be retraced. A State can not be dismembered by Congress. . . . But the people of those States and of every State, actuated by feelings of justice and a regard for our national honor, submit to you the interesting question whether something can not be done, consistently with the rights of States, to preserve this much-injured race.

As a means of effecting this end I suggest for your consideration the propriety of setting apart an ample district west of the Mississippi . . . to be guaranteed to the Indian tribes as long as they shall occupy it. . . . There they may be secured in the enjoyment of governments of their own choice, subject to no other control from the United States than such as may be necessary to preserve peace on the frontier and between the several tribes. There the benevolent may endeavor to teach them the arts of civilization, and, by promoting union and harmony among them, to raise up an interesting commonwealth, destined to perpetuate the race and to attest the humanity and justice of this Government.

This emigration should be voluntary, for it would be cruel and unjust to compel the aborigines to abandon the graves of their fathers and seek a home in a distant land. But they should be distinctly informed that if they remain within the limits of the States they must be subject to their laws. In return for their obedience as individuals they will without doubt be protected in the enjoyment of those possessions which they have improved by their industry. But it seems to me visionary to suppose that in this state of things claims can be allowed on tracts of country on which they have neither dwelt nor made improvements, merely because they have seen them from the mountain or passed them in the chase. Submitting to the laws of the States, and receiving, like other citizens, protection in their persons and property, they will ere long become merged in the mass of our population.

# Indian Removal Is a Dishonorable Policy

*Theodore J. Frelinghuysen*

President Jackson's 1829 proposal for Indian removal was answered by Congress in May 1830 with the Indian Removal Act. The policy of Indian removal was controversial, however, and many congressmen opposed the legislation. One of these congressmen was Senator Theodore J. Frelinghuysen of New Jersey. The selection below is excepted from a six-hour speech he gave before the Senate, filibustering against the Indian Removal Act. Frelinghuysen states that Native American tribes have an unquestionable right to their lands by virtue of having lived on them first. He also points to past agreements that the United States has made, in which U.S. leaders recognized Native Americans' land rights.

As you read, consider the following questions:
1. What political maxim does Frelinghuysen argue is based on "the unchangeable principles of eternal justice"?
2. How does the senator describe the history of relations between white settlers and Native Americans?
3. How did Thomas Jefferson believe the United States should treat American Indians, according to Frelinghuysen?

God, in his providence, planted these tribes on this Western continent, so far as we know, before Great Britain herself had a political existence. I believe, sir, it is not now seriously denied that the Indians are men, endowed with kin-

Excerpted from Theodore J. Frelinghuysen's debate before the United States Congress on the Indian Removal Act, May 1830.

dred faculties and powers with ourselves; that they have a place in human sympathy, and are justly entitled to a share in the common bounties of a benignant Providence. And, with this conceded, I ask in what code of the law of nations, or by what process of abstract deduction, their rights have been extinguished?

Where is the decree or ordinance that has stripped these early and first lords of the soil? Sir, no record of such measure can be found. And I might triumphantly rest the hopes of these feeble fragments of once great nations upon this impregnable foundation. However mere human policy, or the law of power, or the tyrant's pleas of expediency, may have found it convenient at any or in all times to recede from the unchangeable principles of eternal justice, no argument can shake the political maxim, that, where the Indian always has been, he enjoys an absolute right still to be, in the free exercise of his own modes of thought, government and conduct. . . .

## Abusing the Indians' Trust

Our ancestors found these people, far removed from the commotions of Europe, exercising all the rights, and enjoying the privileges, of free and independent sovereigns of this new world. They were not a wild and lawless horde of banditti, but lived under the restraints of government, patriarchal in its character, and energetic in its influence. They had chiefs, head men, and councils. The white men, the authors of all their wrongs, approached them as friends—they extended the olive branch; and, being then a feeble colony and at the mercy of the native tenants of the soil, by presents and professions, propitiated their good will. The Indian yielded a slow, but substantial confidence; granted to the colonists an abiding place; and suffered them to grow up to man's estate beside him. He never raised the claim of elder title: as the white man's wants increased, he opened the hand of his bounty wider and wider. By and by, conditions are changed. His people melt away; his lands are constantly coveted; millions after millions are ceded. The Indian bears it all meekly; he complains, indeed, as well he may; but suffers on: and now he finds that this neighbor, whom his kindness had nourished, has spread an adverse title over the last remains of his patrimony, barely adequate to his wants, and turns upon him, and says, "away! we cannot endure you so near us! These forests and rivers, these groves of your fathers, these firesides and hunting grounds, are ours by the right of power, and the force of numbers." Sir, let every treaty be blotted from our records, and in the judgment of natural and unchangeable truth and justice, I ask, who is the injured, and who is the aggressor? Let conscience answer, and I fear not the result. Sir, let those who please, denounce the public feeling on this subject as the morbid excitement of a false humanity; but I return with the inquiry, whether I have not presented the case truly, with no feature of it overcharged or distorted? And, in view of it, who can help feeling, sir? Do the obligations of justice change with the color of the skin? Is it one of the prerogatives of the white man, that he may disregard the dictates of moral principles, when an Indian shall be concerned? No, sir. In that severe and impartial scrutiny, which futurity will cast over this subject, the righteous award will be, that those very causes which are now pleaded for the relaxed enforcement of the rules of equity, urged upon us not only a rigid execution of the highest justice, to the very letter, but claimed at our hands a generous and magnanimous policy. . . .

## Breaking Our Promises

It is a subject full of grateful satisfaction, that, in our public intercourse with the Indians, ever since the first colonies of white men found an abode on these Western shores, we have distinctly recognized their title; treated with them as owners, and in all our acquisitions of territory, applied ourselves to these ancient proprietors, by purchase and cession alone, to obtain the right of soil. Sir, I challenge the record of any other or different pretension. When, or where, did any assembly or convention meet which proclaimed, or even suggested to these tribes, that the right of discovery contained a superior efficacy over all prior titles?

And our recognition was not confined to the soil merely. We regarded them as nations—far behind us indeed in civilization, but still we respected their forms of government—we conformed our conduct to their notions of civil policy. We were aware of the potency of any edict that sprang from the deliberations of the council fire; and when we desired lands, or peace, or alliances, to this source of power and energy, to this great lever of Indian government we addressed our proposals—to this alone did we look; and from this alone did we expect aid or relief. . . .

Every administration of this Government, from President Washington's, have, with like solemnities and stipulations, held treaties with the Cherokees; treaties, too, by almost all of which we obtained further acquisitions of their territory. Yes, sir, whenever we approached them in the language of friendship and kindness, we touched the chord that won their confidence; and now, when they have nothing left with which to satisfy our cravings, we propose to annul every treaty—to gainsay our word—and, by violence and perfidy, drive the Indian from his home. . . .

## Our Duties Toward the Indians

Mr. Jefferson, in his message to Congress, as early as 1805, and when on the subject of our Indian relations, with his usual enlarged views of public policy, observes: "The aboriginal inhabitants of these countries, I have regarded with the commiseration their history inspires. Endowed with the faculties and the rights of men, breathing an ardent love of liberty and independence, and occupying a country which left them no desire but to be undisturbed, the stream of overflowing population from other regions directed itself on these shores. Without power to divert, or habits to contend against it, they have been overwhelmed by the current, or driven before it. Now, reduced within limits too narrow for the hunter state, humanity enjoins us to teach them agriculture and the domestic arts; to encourage them to that industry, which alone can enable them to maintain their place in existence; and to prepare them in time for that society, which, to bodily comforts, adds the improvement of the mind and morals. We have, therefore, liberally furnished them with the implements of husbandry and household use; we have placed among them instructors in the arts of first necessity; and they are covered with the aegis of the law against aggressors from among ourselves." These, sir, are sentiments worthy of an illustrious statesman. None can fail to perceive the spirit of justice and humanity which Mr. Jefferson cherished towards our Indian allies. He was, through his whole life, the firm unshrinking advocate of their rights, a patron of all their plans for moral improvement and elevation. . . .

I trust, sir, that this brief exposition of our policy, in relation to Indian affairs, establishes, beyond all controversy, the obligation of the United States to protect these tribes in the exercise and enjoyment of their civil and political rights. Sir, the question has ceased to be—What are our duties? An inquiry much more embarrassing is forced upon us: How shall we most plausibly, and with the least possible violence, break our faith? Sir, we repel the inquiry—we reject such an issue—and point the guardians of public honor to the broad, plain . . . [path] of faithful performance, and to which they are equally urged by duty and by interest.

# One Indian's Account of Removal West

*Black Hawk*

The Sauk tribe of what is now Illinois was among the tribes who resisted the policy of Indian removal. In 1804 some members of the tribe had signed a treaty in which they ceded all their lands to white settlers and agreed to move beyond west of the Mississippi. However, a large portion of the Sauk, led by the war chief Black Hawk, never consented to this agreement. In 1831 the army forced Black Hawk's tribe to relocate to Iowa, where they found living conditions difficult. The following year Black Hawk led his followers back to Illinois, where they engaged U.S. troops in a short and bloody conflict that became known as the Black Hawk War. Over one thousand Sauk were killed and Black Hawk was captured and imprisoned.

Black Hawk dictated his biography during his imprisonment. In the passage excerpted below, he describes his efforts to peaceably resist removal and the Sauk's reaction to life west of the Mississippi.

As you read, consider the following questions:
1. Why did Black Hawk feel the Sauk were being forced to move?
2. Under what conditions does the chief say he would have removed peaceably?
3. Based on the text, why do you think Black Hawk insisted on going back to Illinois?

Excerpted from *Life of Black Hawk*, by Black Hawk (Boston: Russell, Odiorne, and Metcalf, 1834).

[In the] fall I paid a visit to the agent, before we started to our hunting grounds, to hear if he had any good news for me. He had news! He said that the land on which our village stood was now ordered to be sold to individuals; and that, when sold, *our right* to remain, by treaty, would be at an end, and that if we returned next spring, we would be *forced* to remove!

We learned during the winter, that part of the lands where our village stood had been sold to individuals, and that the trader at Rock Island had bought the greater part that had been sold. The reason was now plain to me, why he urged us to remove. His object, we thought, was to get our lands. We held several councils that winter to determine what we should do, and resolved, in one of them, to return to our village in the spring, as usual; and concluded, that if we were removed by force, that the trader, agent, and others, must be the cause; and that, if found guilty of having us driven from our village, they should be killed! The trader stood foremost on this list. He had purchased the land on which my lodge stood, and that of our grave yard also! . . .

Our women received bad accounts from the women that had been raising corn at the new village—the difficulty of breaking the new prairie with hoes—and the small quantity of corn raised. We were nearly in the same situation in regard to the latter, it being the first time I ever knew our people to be in want of provision.

I prevailed upon some of Ke-o-kuck's band to return this spring to the Rock river village. Ke-o-kuck [another Sauk leader who had agreed to removal,] would not return with us. I hoped that we would get permission to go to Washington to settle our affairs with our Great Father [the president of the United States]. I visited the agent at Rock Island. He was displeased because we had returned to our village, and told me that we must remove to the west of the Mississippi. I told him plainly that we would not! I visited the interpreter at his house, who advised me to do as the agent had directed me. I then went to see the trader, and upbraided him for buying our lands. He said that if he had not purchased them, some person else would, and that if our Great Father would make an exchange with us, he would willingly give up the land he had purchased to the government. This I thought was fair, and began to think that he had not acted as badly as I had suspected. We again repaired our lodges, and built others, as most of our village had been burnt and destroyed. Our women selected small patches to plant corn (where the whites had not taken them within their fences,) and worked hard to raise something for our children to subsist upon.

I was told that, according to the treaty, we had no right to remain upon the lands sold, and that the government would force us to leave them. There was but a small portion, however, that had been sold; the balance remaining in the hands of the government, we claimed the right (if we had no other) to "live and hunt upon, as long as it remained the property of the government," by a stipulation in the same treaty that required us to evacuate it after it had been sold. This was the land that we wished to inhabit, and thought we had the best right to occupy. . . .

## A Divided People

I would here remark, that our pastimes and sports had been laid aside for the last two years. We were a divided people, forming two parties. Ke-o-kuck being at the head of one, willing to barter our rights merely for the good opinion of the whites; and cowardly enough to desert our village to them. I was at the head of the other party, and was determined to hold on to my village, although I had been ordered to leave it. But, I considered, as myself and band had no agency in selling our country—and that as provision had been made in the treaty, for us all to remain on it as long as it belonged to the United States, that we could not be forced away. I refused, therefore, to quit my village. It was here, that I was born—and here lie the bones of many friends and relations. For this spot I felt a sacred reverence, and never could consent to leave it, without being forced therefrom. . . .

The winter passed off in gloom. We made a bad hunt, for want of the guns, traps, &c. that the whites had taken from our people for whisky! The prospect before us was a bad one. I fasted, and called upon the Great Spirit to direct my steps to the right path. I was in great sorrow—because all the whites with whom I was acquainted, and had been on terms of friendship, advised me so contrary to my wishes, that I begun to doubt whether I had a friend among them.

Ke-o-kuck, who has a smooth tongue, and is a great speaker, was busy in persuading my band that I was wrong—and thereby making many of them dissatisfied with me. I had one consolation—for all the women were on my side, on account of their corn-fields.

On my arrival again at my village, with my band increased, I found it worse than before. . . . In this mood, I called upon the trader, who is fond of talking, and had long been my friend, but now amongst those advising me to give up my village. He received me very friendly, and went on to defend Ke-o-kuck in what he had done, and endeavored to show me that I was bringing distress on our women and children. . . . After thinking some time, I agreed, that I could honorably give up, by being paid for it, according to our customs; but told him, that I could not make the proposal myself, even if I wished, because it would be dishonorable in me to do so. He said he would do it, by sending word to the great chief at St. Louis, that he could remove us peaceably, for the amount stated, to the west side of the Mississippi. A steam boat arrived at the island during my stay. After its departure, the trader told me that he had "requested a war chief [an army officer], who is stationed at Galena, and was on board of the steam boat, to make the offer to the great chief at St. Louis, and that he would soon be back, and bring his answer." I did not let my people know what had taken place, for fear they would be displeased. I did not much like what had been done myself, and tried to banish it from my mind.

After a few days had passed, the war chief returned, and brought for answer, that "the great chief at St. Louis would give us nothing!—and said if we did not remove immediately, we should be drove off!"

# The Decision to Stay

I was not much displeased with the answer brought by the war chief, because I would rather have laid my bones with my forefathers, than remove for any consideration. Yet if a friendly offer had been made, as I expected, I would, for the sake of my women and children, have removed peaceably.

I now resolved to remain in my village, and make no resistance, if the military came, but submit to my fate! I impressed the importance of this course on all my band, and directed them, in case the military came, not to raise an arm against them. . . .

Our women had planted a few patches of corn, which was growing finely, and promised a subsistence for our children—but the white people again commenced ploughing it up!

I now determined to put a stop to it, by clearing our country of the intruders. I went to the principal men and told them, that they must and should leave our country—and gave them until the middle of the next day, to remove in. The worst left within the time appointed—but the one who remained, represented, that his family (which was large,) would be in a starving condition, if he went and left his crop—and promised to behave well, if I would consent to let him remain until fall, in order to secure his crop. He spoke reasonably, and I consented. . . .

The war chief arrived, and convened a council at the agency. Ke-o-kuck and Wà-pel-lo were sent for, and came with a number of their band. The council house was opened, and they were all admitted. Myself and band were then sent for to attend the council. When we arrived at the door, singing a war song, and armed with lances, spears, war clubs and bows and arrows, as if going to battle, I halted, and refused to enter—as I could see no necessity or propriety in having the room crowded with those who were already there. If the council was convened for us, why have others there in our room? The war chief having sent all out, except Ke-o-kuck, Wà-pel-lo, and a few of their chiefs and braves, we entered the council house, in this war-like appearance, being desirous to show the war chief that we were not afraid! He then rose and made a speech.

He said:

"The president is very sorry to be put to the trouble and expense of sending a large body of soldiers here, to remove you from the lands you have long since ceded to the United States. Your Great Father has already warned you repeatedly, through your agent, to leave the country; and he is very sorry to find that you have disobeyed his orders. Your Great Father wishes you well; and asks nothing from you but what is reasonable and right. I hope you will consult your own interest, and leave the country you are occupying, and go to the other side of the Mississippi."

I replied: "That we had never sold our country. We never received any annuities from our American father! And we are determined to hold on to our village!"

The war chief, apparently angry, rose and said:—"Who is Black Hawk? Who is Black Hawk?"

I responded:

"I am a SAC! [an alternative spelling of Sauk] my forefather was a SAC! and all the nations call me a SAC!!"

The war chief said:

"I came here, neither to beg nor hire you to leave your village. My business is to remove you, peaceably if I can, but forcibly if I must! I will now give you two days to remove in—and if you do not cross the Mississippi within that time, I will adopt measures to force you away!"

I told him that I never could consent to leave my village, and was determined not to leave it! . . .

## Forced Removal

All our plans were now defeated. We must cross the river, or return to our village and await the coming of the war chief with his soldiers. We determined on the latter: but finding that our agent, interpreter, trader, and Ke-o-kuck (who were determined on breaking my ranks,) had seduced several of my warriors to cross the Mississippi, I sent a deputation to the agent, at the request of my band, pledging myself to leave the country in the fall, provided permission was given us to remain, and secure our crop of corn, then growing—as we would be in a starving situation if we were driven off without the means of subsistence.

The deputation returned with an answer from the war chief, "that no further time would be given us than that specified, and if we were not then gone, he would remove us!"

I directed my village crier to proclaim, that my orders were, in the event of the war chief coming to our village to remove us, that not a gun should be fired, nor any resistance offered. That if he determined to fight, for them to remain quietly in their lodges, and let him kill them if he chose! . . .

Some of our young men who had been out as spies, came in and reported, that they had discovered a large body of mounted men coming towards our village, who looked like a war party. They arrived, and took a position below Rock river, for their place of encampment. The great war chief entered Rock river in a steam-boat, with his soldiers and one big gun! . . .

The war chief appointed the next day to remove us! I would have remained and been taken prisoner by the regulars, but was afraid of the multitude of pale faces, who were on horseback, as they were under no restraint of their chiefs.

We crossed the Mississippi during the night, and encamped some distance below Rock Island. The great war chief convened another council, for the purpose of making a treaty with us. In this treaty he agreed to give us corn in place of that we had left growing in our fields. I touched the goose-quill to this treaty, and was determined to live in peace.

The corn that had been given us, was soon found to be inadequate to our wants; when loud lamentations were heard in the camp, by our women and children, for their roasting-ears, beans, and squashes. To satisfy them, a small party of braves went over, in the night, to steal corn from their own fields. They were discovered by the whites, and fired upon. Complaints were again made of the depredations committed by some of my people, on their own corn-fields!

# The Battle of Sand Creek Was a Great Victory Against the Indians

Rocky Mountain News

One of the most controversial clashes in the North American Wars of the nineteenth century occurred on November 29, 1864, at the Sand Creek reservation in Colorado. After a series of Indian raids on ranches in the area, Cheyenne chief Black Kettle had met with army officers in Denver and surrendered himself and his tribe as prisoners of war. Shortly after Black Kettle returned to the Sand Creek reservation, however, Colonel John M. Chivington and approximately 700 Colorado volunteers attacked the reservation. Some of the approximately 500 Cheyenne and Arapaho at the reservation fled, but many of the slowest-moving dug into excavated pits and trenches for protection, where, over the course of several hours, they were shot at and shelled by Chivington and his men. At least 150 Indians were killed, many of them women, children, and the elderly.

Excerpted below is one of the earliest newspaper accounts of the incident. In praising Chivington and his men and applauding the devastating blow they have dealt the Cheyenne and Arapaho, the Colorado *Rocky Mountain News* account demonstrates the anti-Indian sentiment prevalent at the time. Not until months later, when congressional investigations revealed the atrocities committed at Sand Creek, was Chivington's "victory" condemned as a massacre.

Excerpted from "The Battle of Sand Creek," *Rocky Mountain News*, 1864.

As you read, consider the following questions:

1. How does the *Rocky Mountain News* describe the defense that the Indians' mounted?
2. What aspects of the Chivington victory does the author single out for praise?

---

Among the brilliant feats of arms in Indian warfare, the recent campaign of our Colorado volunteers will stand in history with few rivals, and none to exceed it in final results. We are not prepared to write its history, which can only be done by some one who accompanied the expedition, but we have gathered from those who participated in it and from others who were in that part of the country, some facts which will doubtless interest many of our readers.

The people of Colorado are well aware of the situation occupied by the third regiment during the great snowstorm which set in the last of October. Their rendezvous was in Bijou Basin, about eighty miles southeast of this city, and close up under the foot of the Divide. That point had been selected as the base for an Indian campaign. Many of the companies reached it after the storm set in; marching for days through the driving, blinding clouds of snow and deep drifts. Once there, they were exposed for weeks to an Arctic climate, surrounded by a treeless plain covered three feet deep with snow. Their animals suffered for food and with cold, and the men fared but little better. They were insufficiently supplied with tents and blankets, and their sufferings were intense. At the end of a month the snow had settled to the depth of two feet, and the command set out upon its long contemplated march. The rear guard left the Basin on the 23rd of November. Their course was southeast, crossing the Divide and thence heading for Fort Lyon. For one hundred miles the snow was quite two feet in depth, and for the next hundred it ranged from six to twelve inches. Beyond that the ground was almost bare and the snow no longer impeded their march.

On the afternoon of the 28th the entire command reached

Fort Lyon, a distance of two hundred and sixty miles, in less than six days, and so quietly and expeditiously had the march been made that the command at the fort was taken entirely by surprise. When the vanguard appeared in sight in was reported that a body of Indians were approaching, and precautions were taken for their reception. No one upon the route was permitted to go in advance of the column, and persons who it was suspected would spread the news of the advance were kept under surveillance until all danger from that source was past.

## The Attack

At Fort Lyon the force was strengthened by about two hundred and fifty men of the first regiment, and at nine o'clock in the evening the command set out for the Indian village. The course was due north, and their guide was the Polar star. As daylight dawned they came in sight of the Indian camp, after a forced midnight march of forty-two miles, in eight hours, across the rough, unbroken plain. But little time was required for preparation. The forces had been divided and arranged for battle on the march, and just as the sun rose they dashed upon the enemy with yells that would put a Comanche army to blush. Although utterly surprised, the savages were not unprepared, and for a time their defense told terribly against our ranks. Their main force rallied and formed in line of battle on the bluffs beyond the creek, where they were protected by rudely constructed rifle-pits, from which they maintained a steady fire until the shells from company C's (third regiment) howitzers began dropping among them, when they scattered and fought each for himself in genuine Indian fashion. As the battle progressed the field of carriage widened until it extended over not less than twelve miles of territory. The Indians who could escaped or secreted themselves, and by three o'clock in the afternoon the carnage had ceased. It was estimated that between three and four hundred of the savages got away with their lives. Of the balance there were neither wounded nor prisoners. Their strength at the beginning of the action was estimated at nine hundred.

Their village consisted of one hundred and thirty Cheyenne and with Arapahoe lodges. These, with their contents, were totally destroyed. Among their effects were large supplies of flour, sugar, coffee, tea, &c. Women's and children's clothing were found; also books and many other articles which must have been taken from captured trains or houses. One white man's scalp was found which had evidently been taken but a few days before. The Chiefs fought with unparalleled bravery, falling in front of their men. One of them charged alone against a force of two or three hundred, and fell pierced with balls far in advance of his braves.

Our attack was made by five battalions. The first regiment, Colonel Chivington, part of companies C, D, E, G, H and K, numbering altogether about two hundred and fifty men, was divided into two battalions; the first under command of Major Anthony, and the second under Lieutenant Wilson, until the latter was disabled, when the command devolved upon Lieutenant Dunn. The three battalions of the third, Colonel Shoup, were led, respectively, by Lieutenant Colonel Bowen, Major Sayr, and Captain Cree. The action was begun by the battalion of Lieutenant Wilson, who occupied the right, and by a quick and bold movement cut off the enemy from their herd of stock. From this circumstance we gained our great advantage. A few Indians secured horses, but the great majority of them had to fight or fly on foot. Major Anthony was on the left, and the third in the centre.

Among the killed were all the Cheyenne chiefs, Black Kettle, White Antelope, Little Robe, Left Hand, Knock Knee, One Eye, and another, name unknown. Not a single prominent man of the tribe remains, and the tribe itself is almost annihilated. The Arapahoes probably suffered but little. It has been reported that the chief Left Hand, of that tribe, was killed, but Colonel Chivington is of the opinion that he was not. Among the stock captured were a number of government horses and mules, including the twenty or thirty stolen from the command of Lieutenant Chase at Jimmy's camp last summer.

The Indian camp was well supplied with defensive works. For half a mile along the creek there was an almost continuous chain of rifle-pits, and another similar line of works crowned the adjacent bluff. Pits had been dug at all the salient points for miles. After the battle twenty-three dead Indians were taken from one of these pits and twenty-seven from another.

## Covered with Glory

Whether viewed as a march or as a battle, the exploit has few, if any, parallels. A march of 260 miles in but a fraction more than five days, with deep snow, scanty forage, and no road, is a remarkable feat, whilst the utter surprise of a large Indian village is unprecedented. In no single battle in North America, we believe, have so many Indians been slain.

It is said that a short time before the command reached the scene of battle of an old squaw partially alarmed the village by reporting that a great herd of buffalo were coming. She heard the rumbling of the artillery and tramp of the moving squadrons, but her people doubted. In a little time the doubt was dispelled, but not by buffaloes.

A thousand incidents of individual daring and the passing events of the day might be told, but space forbids. We leave the task for eye-witnesses to chronicle. All acquitted themselves well, and Colorado soldiers have again covered themselves with glory.

# The Sand Creek Massacre Was a Tragedy

*George Bent*

George Bent was a half-Cheyenne who was living at Sand Creek in November 1864, when Colonel John Chivington and his troops attacked the reservation. In this account of the massacre, given a few years after the event, Bent describes the chaos and confusion that accompanied the attack. Some Indians were killed in the initial attack, according to Bent, while others were shot by the soldiers after they had been captured and still others froze to death after fleeing their homes.

As you read, consider the following questions:
1. How did Black Kettle initially respond to the troops' arrival, according to Bent?
2. By Bent's estimate, what proportion of those killed in the massacre were women and children?
3. What does the author believe was Chivington's goal in the attack?

---

When I looked toward the chief's lodge, I saw that Black Kettle had a large American flag up on a long lodgepole as a signal to the troop that the camp was friendly. Part of the warriors were running out toward the pony herds and the rest of the people were rushing about the camp in great fear. All the time Black Kettle kept calling out not to be frightened; that the camp was under protection and there was no danger. Then suddenly the troops opened fire on this mass of men, women, and children, and all began to scatter and run.

Excerpted from "An Eyewitness Report of the Sand Creek Massacre," by George Bent, *The Fighting Cheyennes*, edited by George Bird Grinnell (New York: C. Scribner's Sons, 1915).

The main body of Indians rushed up the bed of the creek, which was dry, level sand with only a few little pools of water here and there. On each side of this wide bed stood banks from two to ten feet high. While the main body of the people fled up this dry bed, a part of the young men were trying to save the herd from the soldiers, and small parties were running in all directions toward the sand hills. One of these parties, made up of perhaps ten middle-aged Cheyenne men, started for the sand hills west of the creek, and I joined them. Before we had gone far, the troops saw us and opened a heavy fire on us, forcing us to run back and take shelter in the bed of the creek. We now started up the stream bed, following the main body of Indians and with a whole company of cavalry close on our heels shooting at us every foot of the way. As we went along we passed many Indians, men, women, and children, some wounded, others dead, lying on the sand and in the pools of water. Presently we came to a place where the main party had stopped, and were now hiding in pits that they had dug in the high bank of the stream. Just as we reached this place, I was struck by a ball in the hip and badly wounded, but I managed to get into one of the pits. About these pits nearly all Chivington's men had gathered and more were continually coming up, for they had given up the pursuit of the small bodies of Indians who had fled to the sand hills.

## The Slaughter

The soldiers concentrated their fire on the people in the pits, and we fought back as well as we could with guns and bows, but we had only a few guns. The troops did not rush in and fight hand to hand, but once or twice after they had killed many of the men in a certain pit, they rushed in and finished up the work, killing the wounded and the women and children that had not been hurt. The fight here was kept up until nearly sundown, when at last the commanding officer called off his men and all started back down the creek toward the camp that they had driven us from. As they went back, the soldiers scalped the dead lying in the bed of the stream and cut up the bodies in a manner that no Indian could equal. Little Bear told me recently that after the fight he saw the soldiers scalping the dead and saw an old woman who had been scalped by the soldiers walk about, but unable to see where to go. Her whole scalp had been taken and the skin of her forehead fell down over her eyes.

At the beginning of the attack Black Kettle, with his wife and White Antelope, took their position before Black Kettle's lodge and remained there after all others had left the camp. At last Black Kettle, seeing that it was useless to stay longer, started to run, calling out to White Antelope to follow him, but White Antelope refused and stood there ready to die, with arms folded, singing his death song:

Nothing lives long,
Except the earth and the mountains,

until he was shot down by the soldiers. Black Kettle and his wife followed the Indians in their flight up the dry bed of the creek. The soldiers pursued them, firing at them constantly, and before the two had gone far, the woman was shot down. Black Kettle supposed she was dead and, the soldiers being close behind him, continued his flight. The troops followed him all the way to the rifle pits, but he reached them unhurt. After the fight he returned down the stream looking for his wife's body. Presently he found her alive and not dangerously wounded. She told him that after she had fallen wounded, the soldiers had ridden up and again shot her several times as she lay there on the sand. Black Kettle put her on his back and carried her up the stream until he met a mounted man, and the two put her on the horse. She was taken to the Cheyenne camp on Smoky Hill. When she reached there, it was found that she had nine wounds on her body. My brother Charlie was in the camp, and he and Jack Smith, another half blood, were captured. After the fight the soldiers took Jack Smith out and shot him in cold blood. Some of the officers told Colonel

Chivington what the men were about and begged him to save the young man, but he replied curtly that he had given orders to take no prisoners and that he had no further orders to give. Some of the soldiers shot Jack and were going to shoot my brother also, but fortunately among the troops there were a number of New Mexican scouts whom Charlie knew, and these young fellows protected him. A few of our women and children were captured by the soldiers, but were turned over to my father at the fort, with the exception of two little girls and a boy, who were taken to Denver and there exhibited as great curiosities.

## The Wounded Flee

Soon after the troops left us, we came out of the pits and began to move slowly up the stream. More than half of us were wounded and all were on foot. When we had gone up the stream a few miles, we began to meet some of our men who had left camp at the beginning of the attack and tried to save the horses which were being driven off by the soldiers. None of these men had more than one rope, so each one could catch only a single horse. As they joined us, the wounded were put on these ponies' backs. Among these men was my cousin, a young Cheyenne, from whom I secured a pony. I was so badly wounded that I could hardly walk.

When our party had gone about ten miles above the captured camp, we went into a ravine and stopped there for the night. It was very dark and bitterly cold. Very few of us had warm clothing, for we had been driven out of our beds and had had no time to dress. The wounded suffered greatly. There was no wood to be had, but the unwounded men and women collected grass and made fires. The wounded were placed near the fires and covered with grass to keep them from freezing. All night long the people kept up a constant hallooing to attract the attention of any Indians who might be wandering about in the sand hills. Our people had been scattered all over the country by the troops, and no one knows how many of them may have been frozen to death in the open country that night.

We left this comfortless ravine before day and started east toward a Cheyenne camp on the Smoky Hill, forty or fifty miles away. The wounded were all very stiff and sore, and could hardly mount. My hip was swollen with the cold, and I had to walk a long way before I could mount my horse. Not only were half our party wounded, but we were obliged also to look out for a large number of women and little children. In fact, it was on the women and children that the brunt of this terrible business fell. Over three-fourths of the people killed in the battle were women and children.

We had not gone far on our way before we began to meet Indians from the camp on the Smoky Hill. They were coming, bringing us horses, blankets, cooked meat, and other supplies. A few of our people had succeeded in getting horses when the soldiers began the attack, and these men had ridden to the Smoky Hill River and sent aid back to us from the camp there. Almost everyone in that camp had friends or relatives in our camp, and when we came in sight of the lodges, everyone left the camp and came out to meet us, wailing and mourning in a manner that I have never heard equaled.

A year after this attack on our camp a number of investigations of the occurrence were made. Colonel Chivington's friends were then extremely anxious to prove that our camp was hostile, but they had no facts in support of their statements. It was only when these investigations were ordered that they began to consider the question; at the time of the attack it was of no interest to them whether we were hostiles or friendlies. One of Chivington's most trusted officers recently said: "When we came upon the camp on Sand Creek we did not care whether these particular Indians were friendly or not." It was well known to everybody in Denver that the Colonel's orders to his troops were to kill Indians, to "kill all, little and big."

# An Eyewitness at the Battle of Little Big Horn

*Two Moons*

In June 1876, the U.S. Army was sent to the Montana Territory to remove the Dakota Indians in the area and to make way for miners in search of gold. In the famous Battle of Little Big Horn, also known as Custer's Last Stand, General George Custer led a failed U.S. Cavalry attack against a large group of Cheyenne and Sioux that were camped in the territory. Custer was quickly surrounded and in little more than an hour he and two hundred of the men in his command were dead. The Battle of Little Big Horn shocked the United States. It was one of the most stunning victories in the Native Americans' long struggle against white encroachment. However, it was short-lived: Within a few years the Plain tribes had no choice but to surrender.

Two Moons was a Cheyenne chief who joined with Lakota chief Crazy Horse and his people in the attack after being left homeless by an army raid. The following document is his account of the Battle of Little Big Horn—or the Battle of Greasy Grass, as it is known to Native Americans. This dramatic account illustrates the hectic pace of the battle.

As you read, consider the following questions:
1. Who initiated the battle, according to Two Moons?
2. Based on Two Moons's account, does it seem like the battle took a long time?

I went to water my horses at the creek, and washed them off with cool water, then took a swim myself. I came back

Excerpted from "The Battle of Greasy Grass," by Two Moons, *McClure's Magazine*, 1898.

to the camp afoot. When I got near my lodge, I looked up the Little Horn towards Sitting Bull's camp. I saw a great dust rising. It looked like a whirlwind. Soon Sioux horseman came rushing into camp shouting: "Soldiers come! Plenty white soldiers."

I ran into my lodge, and said to my brother-in-law, "Get your horses; the white man is coming. Everybody run for horses."

Outside, far up the valley, I heard a battle cry, Hay-ay, hay-ay! I heard shooting, too, this way [clapping his hands very fast]. I couldn't see any Indians. Everybody was getting horses and saddles. After I had caught my horse, a Sioux warrior came again and said, "Many soldiers are coming."

Then he said to the women, "Get out of the way, we are going to have hard fight."

I said, "All right, I am ready."

I got on my horse, and rode out into my camp. I called out to the people all running about: "I am Two Moons, your chief. Don't run away. Stay here and fight. You must stay and fight the white soldiers. I shall stay even if I am to be killed."

I rode swiftly toward Sitting Bull's camp. There I saw the white soldiers fighting in a line. Indians covered the flat. They began to drive the soldiers all mixed up—Sioux, then soldiers, then more Sioux, and all shooting. The air was full of smoke and dust. I saw the soldiers fall back and drop into the river-bed like buffalo fleeing. They had no time to look for a crossing. The Sioux chased them up the hill, where they met more soldiers in wagons, and then messengers came saying more soldiers were going to kill the women, and the Sioux turned back. Chief Gall was there fighting, Crazy Horse also.

I then rode toward my camp, and stopped squaws from carrying off lodges. While I was sitting on my horse I saw flags come up over the hill to the east like that [he raised his fingertips]. Then the soldiers rose all at once, all on horses, like this [he put his fingers behind each other to indicate that Custer appeared marching in columns of fours]. They formed into three bunches [squadrons] with a little ways between. Then a bugle sounded, and they all got off horses, and some soldiers led the horses back over the hill.

## The Stand

Then the Sioux rode up the ridge on all sides, riding very fast. The Cheyennes went up the left way. Then the shooting was quick, quick. Pop-pop-pop very fast. Some of the soldiers were down on their knees, some standing. Officers all in front. The smoke was like a great cloud, and everywhere the Sioux went the dust rose like smoke. We circled all round him—swirling like water round a stone. We shoot, we ride fast, we shoot again. Soldiers drop, and horses fall on them. Soldiers in line drop, but one man rides up and down the line—all the time shouting. He rode a sorrel horse with white face and white fore-legs. I don't know who he was. He was a brave man.

Indians keep swirling round and round, and the soldiers killed only a few. Many soldiers fell. At last all horses killed but five. Once in a while some man would break out and run toward the river, but he would fall. At last about a hundred men and five horsemen stood on the hill all bunched together. All along the bugler kept blowing his commands. He was very brave too. Then a chief was killed. I hear it was Long Hair [Custer], I don't know; and then the five horsemen and the bunch of men, may be so forty, started toward the river. The man on the sorrel horse led them, shouting all the time. He wore a buckskin shirt, and had long black hair and mustache. He fought hard with a big knife. His men were all covered with white dust. I couldn't tell whether they were officers or not. One man all alone ran far down toward the river, then round up over the hill. I thought he was going to escape, but a Sioux fired and hit him in the head. He was the last man. He wore braid on his arms [sergeant].

All the soldiers were now killed, and the bodies were stripped. After that no one could tell which were officers. The bodies were left where they fell. We had no dance that night. We were sorrowful.

Next day four Sioux chiefs and two Cheyennes and I, Two Moons, went upon the battlefield to count the dead. One man carried a little bundle of sticks. When we came to dead men, we took a little stick and gave it to another man, so we counted the dead. There were 388. There were thirty-nine Sioux and seven Cheyennes killed, and about a hundred wounded.

Some white soldiers were cut with knives, to make sure they were dead; and the war women had mangled some. Most of them were left just where they fell. We came to the man with the big mustache; he lay down the hills towards the river. The Indians did not take his buckskin shirt. The Sioux said, "That is a big chief. That is Long Hair." I don't know. I had never seen him. The man on the white-faced horse was the bravest man.

That day as the sun was getting low our young men came up the Little Horn riding hard. Many white soldiers were coming in a big boat, and when we looked we could see the smoke rising. I called my people together, and we hurried up the Little Horn, into Rotten Grass Valley. We camped there three days, and then rode swiftly back over our old trail to the east. Sitting Bull went back into the Rosebud and down the Yellowstone, and away to the north. I did not see him again.

# Americans React to Custer's Defeat

New York Times

The Battle of Little Big Horn shocked the United States. People in the East learned of the battle on July 6, 1876, shortly after the country's centennial. In the article excerpted below, the *New York Times* discusses the causes and consequences of Custer's disastrous operation. The *New York Times* describes the Sioux as being much fiercer than other tribes the U.S. Army has fought. According to the newspaper, there is a growing feeling among congressional leaders that the "red devils" of the West must be vanquished once and for all, but the government is unsure how to fund a new, large-scale offensive against the Sioux.

As you read, consider the following questions:
1. What is the "immediate" cause of the disaster, according to the *Times*?
2. How does the author contrast the Sioux with the Indians of the Southwest?
3. What obstacles are there to a renewed campaign against the Sioux, according to the *Times*?

Washington, July 6.—The news of the fatal charge of Gen. Custer and his command against the Sioux Indians has caused great excitement in Washington, particularly among Army people and about the Capitol. The first impulse was to doubt the report, or set it down as some heartless hoax or at least a greatly exaggerated story by some frightened fugitive. At the second thought the report was generally ac-

Excerpted from "Fruits of the Ill-Advised Black Hills Expedition of Two Years Ago," *New York Times*, July 1876.

cepted as true in its chief and appalling incidents. The campaign against the wild Sioux was undertaken under disadvantageous circumstances owing to the refusal of Congress to appropriate money for the establishment of military posts on the upper Yellowstone River. Gen. Sherman and Gen. Sheridan both asked for these posts, which, in case of anticipated troubles would give the troops a base of supplies about four hundred miles nearer the hostile country than they could otherwise have. The posts desired would have been accessible by steamboats on the Yellowstone, which would have conveyed men and supplies. The House Committee on Military Affairs unanimously recommended their establishment, but the Committee on Appropriations refused to provide in their bills the necessary means. This is regarded as the immediate cause of the disaster. The remote cause was undoubtedly the expedition into the Black Hills two years ago in violation of laws and treaties, authorized by Secretary Belknap and led by Gen. Custer. If there had been a post at the head of navigation on the Yellowstone the expedition would doubtless have proceeded thence against the Indians in one invincible column. The policy of sending three converging columns so many hundred miles against such brave and skillful soldiers as the Sioux has been the cause of some uneasiness here among the few who have taken the trouble to think about the facts and prospects. The Sioux seem to have understood clearly the plan of attack, and threw themselves with their whole force first against Gen. Crook's column and now against Custer's, and both times inflicted serious disaster. The feeling was common today that the campaign is a failure, and that there must follow a general Indian war, promising to be costly in men and money. The Sioux are a distinct race of men from the so-called Indians of the Southwest, among whom the army found such easy work two and three years ago. The Sioux live by the chase and feed chiefly upon flesh.

The Southern Indians are farmers and eat fruits and vegetables, the latter are at their worst cruel, cowardly robbers. The former are as much like the brave and warlike red men representing by *The Last of the Mohicans* as ever existed outside the covers of fiction and romance. This difference between the foes in the North and Southwest seems not to have been well counted upon, nor provided for, and formed, as it might, prudently, no restraint upon the reckless fatal charge of the 300. If the tale told by the courier Taylor is true, the charge has scarce a parallel in the history of civilized or savage warfare.

The massacre of Major Dade and his command in the Florida war is alone comparable with it in American history. The reason for an expedition against the Indians this Summer is not well understood, nor has any satisfactory explanation been published. The wild Sioux had never been willing to live upon the reservations marked out for them, and the understanding has been that they were to be whipped into submission, and compelled to live like Red Cloud and Spotted Tail, with their bands, about the Government agencies. The question of the policy and right of the war will now be renewed and discussed, and, indeed, is discussed today. Those who believe in the policy of the extermination of the Indians, and think the speedier the better its accomplishment, look upon the condition of war as inevitable, and are for pouring thousands of troops into the Indian country and giving them a terrible punishment. This class is small, even in the Army, where the policy of extermination is not popular save with a few high and restless officers. The invasion of the Black Hills has been condemned over and over again by the peace party, and there are very many who can truthfully say, "I told you so." From that unwarranted invasion the present difficulties have gradually sprung up, so that an expedition that originally cost a hundred thousand dollars perhaps, must lead to an expenditure of millions, which will advance civilization in no way, except by the destruction of the uncivilized. The Army, if the present campaign wholly fails, is in no condition to renew hostilities with sufficient force, and there is little reason to expect Congress will this session provide for an Indian war. Thus by force of circumstances a continuation of the war would probably be with the Government forces upon the defensive, protecting as far as possible agencies and settlements. There is another result that some hope for. It is the union of the three columns of troops and the delivery of a blow against the Indians that will place them at the mercy of the Army and compel them to sue for peace. The chances are, however, so far as the information now at hand may be relied on, that the Government forces are much too small in number, reduced as they are by two battles, to meet the powerful and exultant Sioux.

# Indians Are an Obstacle to Progress

*Elwell S. Otis*

By the 1870s white settlements could be found throughout the Great Plains, the Southwest, and California. In search of farmland, gold, and other natural resources, whites encroached on the Indians' few remaining lands, and battles between Indians and the U.S. Army became more frequent. In the following excerpt from an 1878 treatise on the "Indian question," Lieutenant Colonel Elwell S. Otis describes Indians as an inferior people and an obstacle to progress.

As you read, consider the following questions:
1. What is Otis's view of Indians' religions, laws, and traditions?
2. What does Otis believe will happen to the Indian race "in a few generations"?

What qualities then does this American Indian lack, that he is so little impressed by the efforts which have been put forth for his amelioration? He has the same physical properties, the same senses, the same elementary mental powers which we possess, but here the parallel ceases. Although equally if not more skilled in the use of the senses than the white man, he lacks the faculty of abstraction, and consequently his imagination, reason and understanding, are of a very low order. He is almost entirely destitute of the moral qualities, and his religious nature is of that kind which presumes the existence of a Supreme Being, simply to account for facts and occurrences beyond his comprehension. His

Excerpted from *The Indian Question*, by Elwell S. Otis (New York: Sheldon and Company, 1878).

conceptions of that Divinity are extremely vague and uncertain. It may be one and indivisible, or it may exist in many and antagonistic forms. . . . His Divinity has none of the attributes of goodness, for he, in his utter ignorance of virtues, is unable to imagine their existence. It is only propitiated by substantial material gifts, and may be persuaded to assist in enterprises of the most wicked character.

## Savage Ways

Like all savage people, the Indian has not the slightest conception of definite law as a rule of action. He is guided by his animal desires. He practices all forms of vice, and even to a great extent those crimes which are pronounced as against nature. He takes little thought except for the present, knows nothing of property in the abstract, and has not therefore any incentive to labor further than to supply immediate wants. Instead of making an effort for moral improvement he strives to strengthen his vicious propensities. He eats the raw liver of ferocious beasts to augment his ferocity, wounds and bruises his person to increase his animal courage, boasts in council of his brutalities, parades them as deeds of approved valor and as examples worthy of imitation.

The brief picture here presented is intended to portray the members of the wild tribes, and is not overdrawn, although they exhibit to us in their superstitious ceremonies and in their councils of state, and even in the hospitalities of their lodges, certain qualities which do not appear to harmonize with the character we have so quickly sketched. It is the manifestation of these traits, such as reverence for the Great Spirit, respect for the dead, affection for those within the family relation, hospitable reception of strangers, admiration for mental endowments, and an occasional display of cunning sagacity and rich imagery of language, which has made the Indian a psychological and metaphysical enigma to many. And indeed to the casual observer of Indian life and manners, our representations would appear paradoxical at best. How shall the seeming inconsistencies be reconciled?

The Indian possesses of course the natural instincts, the general characteristics of humanity, among which is an innate love for kindred and a desire for fellowship. The superstitious observances which attend his mode of worship, if such it can be denominated, the rite of burial, and indeed all religious ceremonies from the sun dance to the exorcism of evil spirits, have been handed down by tradition through countless generations. From whence they proceed, whether borrowed and adapted to circumstances, or whether of native birth and growth, the natural product of the Indian mind, endeavoring to account for existence and cause, cannot be ascertained. So analogous, however, are many of their ceremonies to those practiced in eastern Asia, many centuries ago, so similar are many of their traditions to those long since extant in the old world, that the conclusion is almost forced, that they are in substance of foreign origin. The slaughter of horses over the grave of a relative reminds one of the action of Achilles at the tomb of Patroclus. The act of piercing the ears of children is suggestive of the Jewish rite of circumcision. The conjurations of the medicine man assimilate the sorceries spoken of in ancient history, and the traditions and crude mythology of the Indians, contain much which might be ascribed to the Asiatic pagans.

But from whatever source their ceremonies may be derived, they have become the inheritance of the tribes and have been practiced successive years without variation. They are found to be, when examined, characteristic of those who maintain them, and are attended with cruelty or with a repulsive indelicacy shocking to moral sensibility. Reverence when analyzed becomes a superstitious dread of an unappeased vindictive Deity. The beautiful service of sepulture is an observance repellant to the civilized because of the bloody scenes which accompany it.

The Indian is sometimes called a statesman and an orator. His dignified bearing in council, the beautiful metaphors and rich imagery with which his efforts at oratory often abound, challenge admiration. Language is the embodiment of thought. It mirrors the mind, though it does not reveal intention nor morals. While, therefore, manifestations of the highest excellence which the red man has attained may be witnessed in the proceedings of their great tribal gatherings, no correct opinion of their moral condition can be gained. He is a keen observer of nature, and its objects supply him with figures to illustrate and impress his primitive ideas. With the Indian oratory is an art, the result of study and repeated practice. Few acquire it and they become the leading spirits of the tribe. The maiden speeches of the young chiefs about to assume control of the movements of their people, are generally miserable failures. After a few years of trial some become fluent declaimers and fervent exhorters. Fortunately for their reputations, their ideas are few and simple, and they can by their labor, be frequently reproduced with increased adornment.

The efforts of years secure a dress which is rich and oftentimes brilliant. Still it must be remembered that before the speech obtains our criticism, it is embellished by the imagination of the poetical interpreter.

Considering then fairly the character of the superstitious observances maintained by the Indians, also the nature of their mental productions, neither their devout and religious tendencies, nor their arts and accomplishments, are incompatible with that degree of savagery which is destitute of moral principle and the knowledge of abstract right. These deficiencies, together with that spirit of communism which is prevalent among all tribes, and which is due as well to an undeveloped idea in regard to property, as any desire for common ownership, make the reception and understanding of our American civilization very improbable. . . .

## The Indian's Future

It is well known that no portion of the Indian population can much longer maintain itself after its old customs of life, for wild game can only be found in sufficient quantities for its subsistence in small sections of the country. It is well known that it is impossible to improve the Indian while in a nomadic state, and that in such condition he is a constant source of menace to pioneers, and to the frontier settlements. It is also well known that much of the country now rendered insecure and unremunerative because roamed over by irresponsible tribes, is sought by our citizens for occupation, and that it is desirable that routes of travel be opened through the same which can be safely journeyed over by the public. In fine, it is well understood that imperative necessity and the interests of both races demand, that the entire Indian population shall be permanently located either individually by tribes or collectively, and that it be compelled to conform to the laws of the country. It might also be stated as a fact, that this population must be compelled to work for its food, which must in future be largely gained through agricultural toil, for neither charity, gratitude nor justice, requires the Government to feed it in idleness, and its own well-being and prosperity calls upon it to labor for its own maintenance and support.

The question of the future relationship of the white and red races to each other, cannot be satisfactorily determined. Very likely, the idea that a large civilized Indian nation might be created, and preserved, within the country, has been entirely abandoned. That has given way to the hope that Indian communities may be perpetuated, and made similar, in action and intention, to white societies. Speculation, however, based upon tendencies as shown in the past, might lead to the belief that such a hope cannot be realized.

## Gradual Absorption

We have in mind more particularly, that gradual absorption of the Indian stock, which has been in progress since the discovery of America, and which is even more noticeable in Mexico, and in some of the South American provinces, than in the United States. But even with us, it has been so rapidly progressing, as to raise a strong presumption, that the Indian race will, in a few generations, be practically absorbed. In eighteen hundred and seventy-six, the Commissioner of Indian Affairs reported, that nearly one-sixth of the Indian population of the United States, exclusive of Alaska, was made up of mixed bloods; and his figures show, that only about one half of the Cherokees, Creeks, Choctaws, Chickasaws and Seminoles are of pure extraction. These estimates are approximative, and really enumerate the mixed bloods at too low a rate. At many of the agencies, a large number of the half and quarter breeds there dwelling seem to be almost entirely ignored.

The gradual absorption of our Indian stock will assuredly continue, and it is probable, that it will be finally merged in the great body of our white population. The question whether the unity of the two races will produce vigorous physical organisms, is still debatable; and the psychological inquiry, whether the product will be mentally and morally of an inferior order, is still unsettled in the minds of many. Our own opinions upon the latter subject are decided. . . . The cross will be an inferior being, both in mind and morals, when viewed in the light of our civilization, or rather, when measured by the rules prescribed by our civilization, as tests of nature and quality.

However much such an ultimate result is to be deplored, the effect will scarcely be perceptible upon our institutions, except in those sections of country where the Indians shall have been collected in masses. They are now in numbers, only as one to ninety of our entire white population; and indeed as one to twelve of our colored population. In nineteen hundred, the ratio of Indians to whites, even if the two races can be restrained from much intermingling, will be about as one to one hundred and seventy-five. Whatever view therefore, may be taken of this social problem no decided effect can be produced upon our national character. It is only in the event that Indians are collected in large bodies (which certainly, in so far as attempted, seems to have encouraged amalgamation) that any danger is to be apprehended. Should a course of action, having for its object the concentration of the tribes, be persistently and successfully prosecuted, we shall have, within the heart of the United States, an element which will there prolong social disorder for generations to come. If scattered throughout the interior, its evil effects will, in a short time, be neutralized.

# Indians Want to Live in Peace with Whites

*Chief Joseph*

In 1875 the U.S. Army went to war with the Nez Percé of eastern Oregon, who were led by Young Joseph. Chief Joseph and most of his tribe were captured in 1877 and forced onto a reservation in Oklahoma. In 1879 Chief Joseph made a trip to Washington, D.C., where he made a speech calling on the government to rethink its Indian policies. In the excerpts below, Chief Joseph recounts the tragic decline of his tribe since its first contact with Europeans and the battles his people fought in the face of American westward expansion.

As you read, consider the following questions:
1. What is Chief Joseph's view of white men's trustworthiness?
2. According to the chief, what wrongs were committed against his tribe, which eventually led to war between the Nez Percé and the U.S. Army?
3. How does Chief Joseph feel the U.S. government should treat Indians?

My friends, I have been asked to show you my heart. I am glad to have a chance to do so. I want the white people to understand my people. Some of you think an Indian is like a wild animal. This is a great mistake. I will tell you all about our people, and then you can judge whether an Indian is a man or not. I believe much trouble and blood would be saved if we opened our hearts more. I will tell

Excerpted from "An Indian's View of Indian Affairs," by Young Joseph, *North American Review*, April 1879.

you in my way how the Indian sees things. The white man has more words to tell you how they look to him, but it does not require many words to speak the truth. What I have to say will come from my heart, and I will speak with a straight tongue. . . .

We did not know there were other people besides the Indian until about one hundred winters ago, when some men with white faces came to our country. They brought many things with them to trade for furs and skins. They brought tobacco, which was new to us. They brought guns with flint stones on them, which frightened our women and children. Our people could not talk with these white-faced men, but they used signs which all people understand. These men were Frenchmen, and they called our people "Nez Percés," because they wore rings in their noses for ornaments. Although very few of our people wear them now, we are still called by the same name. These French trappers said a great many things to our fathers which have been planted in our hearts. Some were good for us, but some were bad. Our people were divided in opinion about these men. Some thought they taught more bad than good. An Indian respects a brave man, but he despises a coward. He loves a straight tongue, but he hates a forked tongue. . . .

## Wanting Only Peace

For a short time we lived quietly. But this could not last. White men had found gold in the mountains around the land of winding water. They stole a great many horses from us, and we could not get them back because we were Indians. The white men told lies for each other. They drove off a great many of our cattle. Some white men branded our young cattle so they could claim them. We had no friend who would plead our cause before the law councils. It seemed to me that some of the white men in Wallowa were doing these things on purpose to get up a war. They knew that we were not strong enough to fight them. I labored hard to avoid trouble and bloodshed. We gave up some of our country to the white men, thinking that then we could have peace. We were mistaken. The white man would not let us alone. We could have avenged our wrongs many times, but we did not. Whenever the Government has asked us to help them against other Indians, we have never refused. When the white men were few and we were strong we could have killed them all off, but the Nez Percés wished to live at peace. . . .

On account of the treaty made by the other bands of the Nez Percés, the white men claimed my lands. We were troubled greatly by white men crowding over the line. Some of these were good men, and we lived on peaceful terms with them, but they were not all good.

Nearly every year the agent came over from Lapwai [the Idaho reservation to which the Nez Percés had been ordered to move] and ordered us on to the reservation. We always replied that we were satisfied to live in Wallowa. We were careful to refuse the presents or annuities which he offered.

Through all the years since the white men came to Wallowa we have been threatened and taunted by them and the treaty Nez Percés. They have given us no rest. We have had a few good friends among white men, and they have always advised my people to bear these taunts without fighting. Our young men were quick-tempered, and I have had great trouble in keeping them from doing rash things. I have carried a heavy load on my back ever since I was a boy. I learned then that we were but few, while the white men were many, and that we could not hold our own with them. We were like deer. They were like grizzly bears. We had a small country. Their country was large. We were contented to let things remain as the Great Spirit Chief made them. They were not; and would change the rivers and mountains if they did not suit them.

## The Threat of Forced Removal

Year after year we have been threatened, but no war was made upon my people until General [O.O.] Howard came to our country two years ago and told us that he was the white war-chief of all that country. He said: "I have a great many soldiers at my back. I am going to bring them up here, and then I will talk to you again. I will not let white men laugh at me the next time I come. The country belongs to the Government, and I intend to make you go upon the reservation."

I remonstrated with him against bringing more soldiers to the Nez Percés country. He had one house full of troops all the time at Fort Lapwai.

The next spring the agent at Umatilla agency sent an Indian runner to tell me to meet General Howard at Walla Walla. I could not go myself, but I sent my brother and five other head men to meet him, and they had a long talk.

General Howard said: "You have talked straight, and it is all right. You can stay in Wallowa." He insisted that my brother and his company should go with him to Fort Lapwai. When the party arrived there General Howard sent out runners and called all the Indians in to a grand council. I was in that council. I said to General Howard, "We are ready to listen." He answered that he would not talk then, but would hold a council next day, when he would talk plainly. I said to General Howard: "I am ready to talk today. I have been in a great many councils, but I am no wiser. We are all sprung from a woman, although we are unlike in many things. We can not be made over again. You are as you were made, and as you were made you can remain. We are just as we were made by the Great Spirit, and you can not change us; then why should children of one mother and one father quarrel—why should one try to cheat the other? I do not believe that the Great Spirit Chief gave one kind of men the right to tell another kind of men what they must do."

General Howard replied: "You deny my authority, do you? You want to dictate to me, do you?"

Then one of my chiefs—Too-hool-hool-suit—rose in the council and said to General Howard: "The Great Spirit Chief made the world as it is, and as he wanted it, and he made a part of it for us to live upon. I do not see where you get authority to say that we shall not live where he placed us."

General Howard lost his temper and said: "Shut up! I don't want to hear any more of such talk. The law says you shall go upon the reservation to live, and I want you to do so, but you persist in disobeying the law" (meaning the treaty). "If you do not move, I will take the matter into my own hand, and make you suffer for your disobedience."

Too-hool-hool-suit answered: "Who are you, that you ask us to talk, and then tell me I sha'n't talk? Are you the Great Spirit? Did you make the world? Did you make the sun? Did you make the rivers to run for us to drink? Did you make the grass to grow? Did you make all these things, that you talk to us as though we were boys? If you did, then you have the right to talk as you do."

I said: "War can be avoided, and it ought to be avoided. I want no war. My people have always been the friends of the white man. Why are you in such a hurry? I can not get ready to move in thirty days. Our stock is scattered, and Snake River is very high. Let us wait until fall, then the river will be low. We want time to hunt up our stock and gather supplies for winter."

General Howard replied, "If you let the time run over one day, the soldiers will be there to drive you on to the reservation, and all your cattle and horses outside of the reservation at that time will fall into the hands of the white men."

I knew I had never sold my country, and that I had no land in Lapwai; but I did not want bloodshed. I did not want my people killed. I did not want anybody killed. Some of my people had been murdered by white men, and the white murderers were never punished for it. I told General Howard about this, and again said I wanted no war. I wanted the people who lived upon the lands I was to occupy at Lapwai to have time to gather their harvest.

I said in my heart that, rather than have war, I would give up my country. I would give up my father's grave. I would give up everything rather than have the blood of white men upon the hands of my people.

General Howard refused to allow me more than thirty

days to move my people and their stock. I am sure that he began to prepare for war at once. . . .

## Who Is to Blame?

There were bad men among my people who had quarreled with white men, and they talked of their wrongs until they roused all the bad hearts in the council. Still I could not believe that they would begin the war. I know that my young men did a great wrong, but I ask, Who was first to blame? They had been insulted a thousand times; their fathers and brothers had been killed; their mothers and wives had been disgraced; they had been driven to madness by whisky sold to them by white men; they had been told by General Howard that all their horses and cattle which they had been unable to drive out of Wallowa were to fall into the hands of white men; and, added to all this, they were homeless and desperate.

I would have given my own life if I could have undone the killing of white men by my people. I blame my young men and I blame the white men. I blame General Howard for not giving my people time to get their stock away from Wallowa. I do not acknowledge that he had the right to order me to leave Wallowa at any time. I deny that either my father or myself ever sold that land. It is still our land. It may never again be our home, but my father sleeps there, and I love it as I love my mother. I left there, hoping to avoid bloodshed. . . .

My friends among white men have blamed me for the war. I am not to blame. When my young men began the killing, my heart was hurt. Although I did not justify them, I remembered all the insults I had endured, and my blood was on fire. Still I would have taken my people to the buffalo country without fighting if possible. . . .

When I think of our condition my heart is heavy. I see men of my race treated as outlaws and driven from country to country, or shot down like animals.

I know that my race must change. We can not hold our own with the white men as we are. We only ask an even chance to live as other men live. We ask to be recognized as men. We ask that the same law shall work alike on all men. If the Indian breaks the law, punish him by the law. If the white man breaks the law, punish him also.

Let me be a free man—free to travel, free to stop, free to work, free to trade where I choose, free to choose my own teachers, free to follow the religion of my fathers, free to think and talk and act for myself—and I will obey every law, or submit to the penalty.

Whenever the white man treats the Indian as they treat each other, then we will have no more wars. . . .

For this time the Indian race are waiting and praying. I hope that no more groans of wounded men and women will ever go to the ear of the Great Spirit Chief above, and that all people may be one people.

[Hin-mah-too-yah-lat-keht] has spoken for his people.

# 3

# MANIFEST DESTINY

# CHAPTER PREFACE

Relatively few pioneers paid heed to the government's admonitions during the 1820s and 1830s against Americans settling the Indian Territory west of the Mississippi. But the threat of Indian attacks was real, and many would-be westerners chose to avoid the Indian lands of the Midwest. Instead, those who were willing to make the long journey went straight past the Great Plains, all the way to the Pacific Northwest and Oregon Territory. Others chose to settle in Texas, which in the 1820s was a region of Mexico. During the 1840s conflicts surrounding Texas and Oregon made westward expansion the focus of national attention.

Oregon was a concern because England had a partial claim to the region, and the United States was reluctant to provoke war by rejecting the British claim. Nevertheless, during the great migration of 1843, almost two thousand settlers crossed the two thousand miles from Independence, Missouri, to the Willamette Valley. Pressure was mounting on the U.S. government to assert full U.S. control of Oregon by officially annexing the region.

Americans had begun settling in Texas in 1821, when the Mexican government granted Stephen Austin permission to settle three hundred families in the region. The colony quickly grew, and fifteen years later, in 1836, the Republic of Texas declared its independence from Mexico, with Sam Houston as its president. By the early 1840s Americans had begun clamoring for the United States to incorporate Texas into the Union. However, to do so would almost certainly lead to war with Mexico since that country refused to acknowledge Texan independence.

Public pressure to annex both Oregon and Texas was one of the key issues during the U.S. presidential election of 1844, and Democrat James K. Polk won the election by promising to achieve these two goals. With his victory, an expansionist fervor swept the country. This sentiment was given a name in 1845, when Democratic magazine editor John L. O'Sullivan proclaimed the United States' "manifest destiny to overspread the continent allotted by Providence for the free development of our yearly multiplying millions." Soon other Democrats and proponents of westward expansion had taken up the cry of Manifest Destiny.

Manifest Destiny clearly had a religious connotation—that God intended for Americans to "overspread the continent." It also represented a political belief, inherited from the ideology of the Revolution, that American principles of democratic liberalism were destined to be adopted by people everywhere. Finally, appeals to America's Manifest Destiny often had distinct racist undertones, as some leaders proclaimed the white race's "destiny" to overrun American Indians, conquer Mexicans, and subjugate blacks.

# The United States Should Annex Texas

*John L. O'Sullivan*

The idea that the United States should spread its borders across North America had been around since the American Revolution. It was not until 1845, however, that this expansionist impulse was given a name. The phrase *Manifest Destiny* was coined by John L. O'Sullivan, editor of the *Democratic Review*, in an essay justifying the annexation of Texas from Mexico. He used the phrase again in an editorial in the *New York Morning News*, and by 1846 it was a popular slogan among expansionists. In his original 1845 essay, excerpted below, O'Sullivan proclaims America's divine mission to extend its borders all the way to the Pacific, controlling not just Texas but California and Oregon as well.

As you read, consider the following questions:

1. Why, in O'Sullivan's view, is U.S. annexation of Texas justified?
2. Is the author's concept of Manifest Destiny based in part on a belief in white racial superiority? Support your answer with examples from the text.
3. Though construction of the transcontinental railroad did not begin until 1861, support for it grew substantially in the 1840s. How does the transcontinental railroad fit into O'Sullivan's vision for westward expansion?

---

It is time now for opposition to the Annexation of Texas to cease, all further agitation of the waters of bitterness and strife, at least in connexion with this question,—even

Excerpted from "Annexation," by John L. O'Sullivan, *United States Magazine and Democratic Review*, July/August 1845.

though it may perhaps be required of us as a necessary condition of the freedom of our institutions, that we must live on for ever in a state of unpausing struggle and excitement upon some subject of party division or other. But, in regard to Texas, enough has now been given to Party. It is time for the common duty of Patriotism to the Country to succeed;—or if this claim will not be recognized, it is at least time for common sense to acquiesce with decent grace in the inevitable and the irrevocable. . . .

## "Our Manifest Destiny to Overspread the Continent"

Why, were other reasoning wanting, in favor of now elevating this question of the reception of Texas into the Union, out of the lower region of our past party dissensions, up to its proper level of a high and broad nationality, it surely is to be found, found abundantly, in the manner in which other nations have undertaken to intrude themselves into it, between us and the proper parties to the case, in a spirit of hostile interference against us, for the avowed object of thwarting our policy and hampering our power, limiting our greatness and checking the fulfilment of our manifest destiny to overspread the continent, alloted by Providence for the free development of our yearly multiplying millions. This we have seen done by England, our old rival and enemy; and by France, strangely coupled with her against us, under the influence of the Anglicism strongly tinging the policy of her present prime minister, Guizot. The zealous activity with which this effort to defeat us was pushed by the representatives of those governments, together with the character of intrigue accompanying it, fully constituted that case of foreign interference, which Mr. [Senator Henry] Clay himself declared should, and would unite us all in maintaining the common cause of our country against the foreigner and the foe. We are only astonished that this effect has not been more fully and strongly produced, and that the burst of indignation against this unauthorized, insolent and hostile interference against us, has not been more general even among the party before opposed to Annexation, and has not rallied the national spirit and national pride unanimously upon that policy. . . .

It is wholly untrue, and unjust to ourselves, the pretence that the Annexation has been a measure of spoliation, unrightful and unrighteous—of military conquest under forms of peace and law—of territorial aggrandizement at the expense of justice, and justice due by a double sanctity to the weak. This view of the question is wholly unfounded, and has been before so amply refuted in these pages, as well as in a thousand other modes, that we shall not again dwell upon it. The independence of Texas was complete and absolute. It was an independence, not only in fact but of right. No obligation of duty towards Mexico tended in the least degree to restrain our right to effect the desired recovery of the fair province once our own—whatever motives of policy might have prompted a more deferential consideration of her feelings and her pride, as involved in the question. If Texas became people with an American population, it was by no contrivance of our government, but on the express invitation of that of Mexico herself; accompanied with such guaranties of State independence, and the maintenance of a federal system analogous to our own, as constituted a compact fully justifying the strongest measures of redress on the part of those afterwards deceived in this guaranty, and sought to be enslaved under the yoke imposed by its violation. She was released, rightfully and absolutely released, from all Mexican allegiance, or duty of cohesion to the Mexican political body, by the acts and fault of Mexico herself, and Mexico alone. There never was a clearer case. It was not revolution; it was resistance to revolution; and resistance under such circumstances as left independence the necessary resulting state, caused by the abandonment of those with whom her former federal association had existed. What then can be more preposterous than all this clamor by Mexico and the Mexican interest, against Annexation, as a violation of any rights of hers, any duties of ours? . . .

# Not a Pro-Slavery Measure

Nor is there any just foundation for the charge t
ation is a great pro-slavery measure—calculated to me.
and perpetuate that institution. Slavery had nothing to do
with it. Opinions were and are greatly divided, both at the
North and South, as to the influence to be exerted by it on
Slavery and the Slave States. That it will tend to facilitate
and hasten the disappearance of Slavery from all the northern tier of the present Slave States, cannot surely admit of
serious question. The greater value in Texas of the slave labor now employed in those States, must soon produce the
effect of draining off that labor southwardly, by the same
unvarying law that bids water descend the slope that invites it. Every new Slave State in Texas will make at least
one Free State from among those in which that institution
now exists—to say nothing of those portions of Texas on
which slavery cannot spring and grow—to say nothing of
the far more rapid growth of new States in the free West
and Northwest, as these fine regions are overspread by the
emigration fast flowing over them from Europe, as well as
from the Northern and Eastern States of the Union as it exists. On the other hand, it is undeniably much gained for
the cause of the eventual voluntary abolition of slavery,
that it should have been thus drained off towards the only
outlet which appeared to furnish much probability of the
ultimate disappearance of the Negro race from our borders. The Spanish-Indian-American populations of Mexico, Central America and South America, afford the only
receptacle capable of absorbing that race whenever we
shall be prepared to slough it off—to emancipate it from
slavery, and (simultaneously necessary) to remove it from
the midst of our own. Themselves already of mixed and
confused blood, and free from the "prejudices" which
among us so insuperably forbid the social amalgamation
which can alone elevate the Negro race out of a virtually
servile degradation even though legally free, the regions occupied by those populations must strongly attract the black
race in that direction; and as soon as the destined hour of

emancipation shall arrive, will relieve the question of one of its worst difficulties, if not absolutely the greatest. . . .

The country which was the subject of Annexation in this case, from its geographical position and relations, happens to be—or rather the portion of it now actually settled, happens to be—a slave country. But a similar process might have taken place in proximity to a different section of our Union; and indeed there is a great deal of Annexation yet to take place, within the life of the present generation, along the whole line of our northern border. Texas has been absorbed into the Union in the inevitable fulfilment of the general law which is rolling our population westward; the connexion of which with that ratio of growth in population which is destined within a hundred years to swell our numbers to the enormous population of two hundred and fifty millions (if not more), is too evident to leave us in doubt of the manifest design of Providence in regard to the occupation of this continent. It was disintegrated from Mexico in the natural course of events, by a process perfectly legitimate on its own part, blameless on ours; and in which all the censures due to wrong, perfidy and folly, rest on Mexico alone. And possessed as it was by a population which was in truth but a colonial detachment from our own, and which was still bound by myriad ties of the very heart-strings to its old relations, domestic and political, their incorporation into the Union was not only inevitable, but the most natural, right and proper thing in the world— and it is only astonishing that there should be any among ourselves to say it nay. . . .

## From the Atlantic to the Pacific
California will, probably, next fall away from the loose adhesion which, in such a country as Mexico, holds a remote province in a slight equivocal kind of dependence on the metropolis. Imbecile and distracted, Mexico never can exert any real governmental authority over such a country. The impotence of the one and the distance of the other, must make the relation one of virtual independence; unless, by

stunting the province of all natural growth, and forbidding that immigration which can alone develop its capabilities and fulfil the purposes of its creation, tyranny may retain a military dominion which is no government in the legitimate sense of the term. In the case of California this is now impossible. The Anglo-Saxon foot is already on its borders. Already the advance guard of the irresistible army of Anglo-Saxon emigration has begun to pour down upon it, armed with the plough and the rifle, and marking its trail with schools and colleges, courts and representative halls, mills and meeting-houses. A population will soon be in actual occupation of California, over which it will be idle for Mexico to dream of dominion. They will necessarily become independent. All this without agency of our government, without responsibility of our people—in the natural flow of events, the spontaneous working of principles, and the adaptation of the tendencies and wants of the human race to the elemental circumstances in the midst of which they find themselves placed. And they will have a right to independence—to self-government—to the possession of the homes conquered from the wilderness by their own labors and dangers, sufferings and sacrifices—a better and a truer right than the artificial title of sovereignty in Mexico a thousand miles distant, inheriting from Spain a title good only against those who have none better. Their right to independence will be the natural right of self-government belonging to any community strong enough to maintain it—distinct in position, origin and character, and free from any mutual obligations of membership of a common political body, binding it to others by the duty of loyalty and compact of public faith. This will be their title to independence; and by this title, there can be no doubt that the population now fast streaming down upon California will both assert and maintain that independence. Whether they will then attach themselves to our Union or not, is not to be predicted with any certainty. Unless the projected rail-road across the continent to the Pacific be carried into effect, perhaps they may not; though even in that case, the day is not distant when the Empires of the Atlantic and Pacific would again flow together into one, as soon as their inland border should approach each other. But that great work, colossal as appears the plan on its first suggestion, cannot remain long unbuilt. Its necessity for this very purpose of binding and holding together in its iron clasp our fast settling Pacific region with that of the Mississippi valley—the natural facility of the route—the ease with which any amount of labor for the construction can be drawn in from the over-crowded populations of Europe, to be paid in the lands made valuable by the progress of the work itself—and its immense utility to the commerce of the world with the whole eastern coast of Asia, alone almost sufficient for the support of such a road—these considerations give assurance that the day cannot be distant which shall witness the conveyance of the representatives from Oregon and California to Washington within less time than a few years ago was devoted to a similar journey by those from Ohio; while the magnetic telegraph will enable the editors of the "San Francisco Union," the "Astoria Evening Post," or the "Nootka Morning News" to set up in type the first half of the President's Inaugural, before the echoes of the latter half shall have died away beneath the lofty porch of the Capitol, as spoken from his lips.

Away, then, with all idle French talk of balances of power on the American Continent. There is no growth in Spanish America! Whatever progress of population there may be in the British Canadas, is only for their own early severance of their present colonial relation to the little island three thousand miles across the Atlantic; soon to be followed by Annexation, and destined to swell the still accumulating momentum of our progress. And whosoever may hold the balance, though they should cast into the opposite scale all the bayonets and cannon, not only of France and England, but of Europe entire, how would it kick the beam against the simple solid weight of the two hundred and fifty, or three hundred millions—and American millions—destined to gather beneath the flutter of the stripes and stars, in the fast hastening year of the Lord 1945!

# The United States Should Not Annex Texas

*William E. Channing*

In the late 1830s, despite a growing expansionist fervor, there were still many U.S. leaders who opposed expansion in general, and annexation of Texas in particular. In an 1837 letter to Senator Henry Clay, excerpted below, Boston clergyman and Unitarian philosopher William E. Channing outlines the reasons he opposes annexation. Channing argues that annexation would be an inexcusable act of aggression toward Mexico. His letter also demonstrates how the debate over expansion was intertwined with the issue of slavery: Channing and other abolitionists feared that Texas would enter the Union as a slave state (which it did in 1846). Finally, Channing warns that annexation will corrupt the character of the United States, since in his view it represents the triumph of greed and plunder over the principles of freedom and justice.

As you read, consider the following questions:
1. In terms of expansion and conquest, what does Channing say that the annexation of Texas will eventually lead to?
2. According to the author (who wrote this letter twenty-four years before the outbreak of the Civil War), how will the annexation of Texas affect relations between North and South?

---

By this act [the annexation of Texas] our country will enter on a career of encroachment, war, and crime, and will

Excerpted from *The Works of William E. Channing*, by William E. Channing (Boston: J. Munroe, 1848).

merit and incur the punishment and woe of aggravated wrongdoing. The seizure of Texas will not stand alone. It will darken our future history. It will be linked by an iron necessity to long-continued deeds of rapine and blood. Ages may not see the catastrophe of the tragedy, the first scene of which we are so ready to enact. It is strange that nations should be so much more rash than individuals; and this, in the face of experience, which has been teaching, from the beginning of society, that, of all precipitate and criminal deeds, those perpetrated by nations are the most fruitful of misery.

## The Temptation of Conquest

Did this country know itself, or were it disposed to profit by self-knowledge, it would feel the necessity of laying an immediate curb on its passion for extended territory. It would not trust itself to new acquisitions. It would shrink from the temptation to conquest. We are a restless people, prone to encroachment, impatient of the ordinary laws of progress, less anxious to consolidate and perfect than to extend our institutions, more ambitious of spreading ourselves over a wide space than of diffusing beauty and fruitfulness over a narrower field. We boast of our rapid growth, forgetting that, throughout nature, noble growths are slow. Our people throw themselves beyond the bounds of civilization, and expose themselves to relapses into a semibarbarous state, under the impulse of wild imagination, and for the name of great possessions. Perhaps there is no people on earth, on whom the ties of local attachment sit so loosely. . . . It is full time, that we should lay on ourselves serious, resolute restraint. Possessed of a domain, vast enough for the growth of ages, it is time for us to stop in the career of acquisition and conquest. Already endangered by our greatness, we cannot advance without imminent peril to our institutions, union, prosperity, virtue, and peace. Our former additions of territory have been justified by the necessity of obtaining outlets for the population of the South and West. No such pretext exists for the occupation of Texas. We cannot seize upon or join to ourselves that territory, without manifesting and strengthening the purpose of setting no limits to our empire. We give ourselves an impulse, which will and must precipitate us into new invasions of our neighbours' soil. Is it by pressing forward in this course that we are to learn self-restraint? Is cupidity to be appeased by gratification? Is it by unrighteous grasping, that an impatient people will be instructed how to hem themselves within the rigid bounds of justice?

Texas is a country conquered by our citizens; and the annexation of it to our Union will be the beginning of conquests, which, unless arrested and beaten back by a just and kind Providence, will stop only at the Isthmus of Darien. Henceforth, we must cease to cry, Peace, peace. Our Eagle will whet, not gorge its appetite on its first victim; and will snuff a more tempting quarry, more alluring blood, in every new region which opens southward. To annex Texas is to declare perpetual war with Mexico. That word, *Mexico,* associated in men's minds with boundless wealth, has already awakened rapacity. Already it has been proclaimed, that the Anglo-Saxon race is destined to the sway of this magnificent realm, that the rude form of society, which Spain established there, is to yield and vanish before a higher civilization. Without this exposure of plans of rapine and subjugation, the result, as far as our will can determine it, is plain. Texas is the first step to Mexico. The moment we plant our authority on Texas, the boundaries of those two countries will become nominal, will be a little more than lines on the sand of the sea-shore. In the fact, that portions of the Southern and Western States are already threatened with devastation, through the impatience of multitudes to precipitate themselves into the Texan land of promise, we have a pledge and earnest of the flood which will pour itself still further south, when Texas shall be but partially overrun. . . .

It is sometimes said, that nations are swayed by laws, as unfailing as those which govern matter; that they have their destinies; that their character and position carry them forward irresistibly to their goal; that the stationary Turk must sink under the progressive civilization of Russia, as inevitably as the crumbling edifice falls to the earth; that, by alike necessity, the Indians have melted before the white man, and the mixed, degraded race of Mexico must melt before the Anglo-Saxon. Away with this vile sophistry! There is no necessity for crime. There is no Fate to justify rapacious nations, any more than to justify gamblers and robbers, in plunder. We boast of the progress of society, and this progress consists in the substitution of reason and moral principle for the sway of brute force. It is true, that more civilized must always exert a great power over less civilized communities in their neighbourhood. But it may and should be a power to enlighten and improve, not to crush and destroy. We talk of accomplishing our destiny. So did the late conqueror of Europe; and destiny consigned him to a lonely rock in the ocean, the prey of an ambition which destroyed no peace but his own. . . .

## A Vast Field for Slavery

I proceed now to a consideration of what is to me the strongest argument against annexing Texas to the United States. This measure will extend and perpetuate slavery. I have necessarily glanced at this topic in the preceding pages; but it deserves to be brought out distinctly. I shall speak calmly, but I must speak earnestly; and I feel, and rejoice to feel, that, however you may differ from some of my views, yet we do not differ as to the great principle on which all my remarks and remonstrances are founded. Slavery seems to you, as to me, an evil and a wrong. Your language on this subject has given me a satisfaction, for which I owe you thanks; and if, in what I am now to say, I may use expressions which you may think too strong, I am sure your candor will recognise in them the signs of deep conviction, and will acquit me of all desire to irritate or give pain.

The annexation of Texas, I have said, will extend and perpetuate slavery. It is fitted, and, still more, intended to do so. On this point there can be no doubt. As far back as the year

1829, the annexation of Texas was agitated in the Southern and Western States; and it was urged on the ground of the strength and extension it would give the slave-holding interest. . . . Of late the language on this subject is most explicit. The great argument for annexing Texas is, that it will strengthen "the peculiar institutions" of the South, and open a new and vast field for slavery. . . .

The annexation of Texas, if it should be accomplished, would do much to determine the future history and character of this country. It is one of those measures, which call a nation to pause, reflect, look forward, because their force is not soon exhausted. Many acts of government, intensely exciting at the moment, are yet of little importance, because their influence is too transient to leave a trace on history. A bad administration may impoverish a people at home, or cripple its energies abroad, for a year or more. But such wounds heal soon. A young people soon recruits its powers, and starts forward with increased impulse, after the momentary suspension of its activity. The chief interest of a people lies in measures, which, making, perhaps, little noise, go far to fix its character, to determine its policy and fate for ages, to decide its rank among nations. A fearful responsibility rests on those who originate or control these pregnant acts. The destiny of millions is in their hands. The execration of millions may fall on their heads. Long after present excitements shall have passed away, long after they and their generation shall have vanished from the earth, the fruits of their agency will be reaped. Such a measure is that of which I now write. It will commit us to a degrading policy, the issues of which lie beyond human foresight. In opening to ourselves vast regions, through which we may spread slavery, and in spreading it for this, among other ends, that the Slave-holding States may bear rule in the national councils, we make slavery the predominant interest of the state. We make it the basis of power, the spring or guide of public measures, the object for which the revenues, strength, and wealth of the country are to be exhausted. Slavery will be branded on our front, as the great

Idea, the prominent feature of the country. We shall renounce our high calling as a people, and accomplish the lowest destiny to which a nation can be bound. . . .

## A Threat to the Union

I now proceed to another important argument against the annexation of Texas to our country, the argument drawn from the bearings of the measure on our National Union. Next to liberty, union is our great political interest, and this cannot but be loosened, it may be dissolved, by the proposed extension of our territory. I will not say that every extension must be pernicious, that our government cannot hold together even our present confederacy, that the central heart cannot send its influences to the remote States which are to spring up within our present borders. Old theories must be cautiously applied to the institutions of this country. If the Federal government will abstain from minute legislation, and rigidly confine itself within constitutional bounds, it may be a bond of union to more extensive communities than were ever comprehended under one sway. Undoubtedly, there is peril in extending ourselves, and yet the chief benefit of the Union, which is the preservation of peaceful relations among neighbouring States, is so vast, that some risk should be taken to secure it in the greatest possible degree. The objection to the annexation of Texas, drawn from the unwieldiness it would give to the country, though very serious, is not decisive. A far more serious objection is, that it is to be annexed to us for the avowed purpose of multiplying Slave-holding States, and thus giving political power. This cannot, ought not to be borne. It will justify, it will at length demand, the separation of the States. . . .

In other ways the annexation of Texas is to endanger the Union. It will give new violence and passion to the agitation of the question of slavery. It is well known, that a majority at the North have discouraged the discussion of this topic, on the ground, that slavery was imposed on the South by necessity, that its continuance was not of choice, and that the States in which it subsists, if left to themselves, would find a remedy in their own way. Let slavery be systematically proposed as the policy of these States, let it bind them together in efforts to establish political power, and a new feeling will burst forth through the whole North. It will be a concentration of moral, religious, political, and patriotic feelings. The fire, now smothered, will blaze out, and, of consequence, new jealousies and exasperations will be kindled at the South. Strange, that the South should think of securing its "peculiar institutions" by violent means. Its violence necessarily increases the evils it would suppress. For example, by denying the right of petition to those who sought the abolition of slavery within the immediate jurisdiction of the United States, it has awakened a spirit, which will overwhelm Congress with petitions till this right be restored. The annexation of Texas would be a measure of the same injurious character, and would stir up an open, uncompromising hostility to slavery, of which we have seen no example, and which would produce a reaction very dangerous to union. . . .

## A Corrupting Influence

I proceed now to the last head of this communication. I observe, that the cause of Liberty, of free institutions, a cause more sacred than union, forbids the annexation of Texas. It is plain from the whole preceding discussion, that this measure will exert a disastrous influence on the moral sentiments and principles of this country, by sanctioning plunder, by inflaming cupidity, by encouraging lawless speculation, by bringing into the confederacy a community whose whole history and circumstances are adverse to moral order and wholesome restraint, by violating national faith, by proposing immoral and inhuman ends, by placing us as a people in opposition to the efforts of philanthropy, and the advancing movements of the civilized world. It will spread a moral corruption, already too rife among us, and, in so doing, it will shake the foundations of freedom at home, and bring reproach on it abroad. It will be treachery to the great cause which has been confided to this above all nations.

The dependence of freedom on morals is an old subject, and I have no thought of enlarging on the general truth. I wish only to say, that it is one which needs to be brought home to us at the present moment, and that it cannot be trifled with but to our great peril. There are symptoms of corruption amongst us, which show us that we cannot enter on a new career of crime without peculiar hazard. I cannot do justice to this topic without speaking freely of our country, as freely as I should of any other; and unhappily we are so accustomed, as a people, to receive incense, to be soothed by flattery, and to account reputation as a more important interest than morality, that my freedom may be construed into a kind of disloyalty. But it would be wrong to make concessions to this dangerous weakness. I believe that morality is the first interest of a people, and that this requires self-knowledge in nations, as truly as in individuals. He who helps a community to comprehend itself, and to apply to itself a higher rule of action, is the truest patriot, and contributes most to its enduring fame.

I have said, that we shall expose our freedom to great peril by entering on a new career of crime. We are corrupt enough already. In one respect, our institutions have disappointed us all. They have not wrought out for us that elevation of character, which is the most precious, and, in truth, the only substantial blessing of liberty. Our progress in prosperity has indeed been the wonder of the world; but this prosperity has done much to counteract the ennobling influence of free institutions. The peculiar circumstances of the country and of our times have poured in upon us a torrent of wealth; and human nature has not been strong enough for the assault of such severe temptation. Prosperity has become dearer than freedom. Government is regarded more as a means of enriching the country, than of securing private rights. We have become wedded to gain, as our chief good. That, under the predominance of this degrading passion, the higher virtues, the moral independence, the simplicity of manners, the stern uprightness, the self-reverence, the respect for man as man, which are the ornaments and safeguards of a republic, should wither, and give place to selfish calculation and indulgence, to show and extravagance, to anxious, envious, discontented strivings, to wild adventure, and to the gambling spirit of speculation, will surprise no one who has studied human nature. The invasion of Texas by our citizens is a mournful comment on our national morality. Whether without some fiery trial, some signal prostration of our prosperity, we can rise to the force and self-denial of freemen, is a question not easily solved. . . .

## A Nobler Destiny

I have alluded to the want of wisdom with which we are accustomed to speak of our destiny as a people. We are *destined* (that is the word) to overspread North America; and, intoxicated with the idea, it matters little to us how we accomplish our fate. To spread, to supplant others, to cover a boundless space, this seems our ambition, no matter what influence we spread with us. Why cannot we rise to noble conceptions of our destiny? Why do we not feel, that our work as a nation is, to carry freedom, religion, science, and a nobler form of human nature over this continent? and why do we not remember, that to diffuse these blessings we must first cherish them in our own borders; and that whatever deeply and permanently corrupts us will make our spreading influence a curse, not a blessing, to this new world? It is a common idea in Europe, that we are destined to spread an inferior civilization over North America; that our slavery and our absorption in gain and outward interests mark us out, as fated to fall behind the old world in the higher improvements of human nature, in the philosophy, the refinements, the enthusiasm of literature and the arts, which throw a lustre round other countries. I am not prophet enough to read our fate. I believe, indeed, that we are to make our futurity for ourselves. I believe, that a nation's destiny lies in its character, in the principles which govern its policy and bear rule in the hearts of its citizens. I take my stand on God's moral and eternal law. A nation, renouncing and defying this, cannot be free, cannot be great.

# The American People Are Destined to Overrun the Continent

*Thomas Hart Benton*

Thomas Hart Benton, a Democratic senator from Missouri from 1820 to 1851, was a powerful advocate of westward expansion. He was also one of the most eloquent. In the following May 1846 speeches before Congress, Benton advocates the acquisition of Oregon territory from Great Britain. He describes America's Manifest Destiny in grandiose terms, envisioning the United States eventually reaching into Asia. Benton held strong antislavery views, but his speech shows how Manifest Destiny was based on notions of white racial superiority that were popular at the time.

As you read, consider the following questions:
1. What are the advantages of acquiring Oregon, in Benton's view?
2. According to Benton, what divine command has the white race been given, and how has it obeyed?
3. How does Benton describe the fate of the "Red race" (American Indians)?

---

[Oregon] is valuable, both as a country to be inhabited, and as a position to be held and defended. I speak of it, first, as a position, commanding the North Pacific ocean, and overlooking the eastern coast of India. The North Pacific is a rich sea, and is already the seat of a great commerce: British, French, American, Russian, and ships of other nations, fre-

Excerpted from Thomas Hart Benton's speech before the United States Senate, May 22, 25, and 28, 1846.

quent it. Our whaling ships cover it: our ships of war go there to protect our interests; and, great as that interest now is, it is only the beginning. Futurity will develop an immense, and various, commerce on that sea, of which the far greater part will be American. That commerce, neither in the merchant ships which carry it on, nor in the military marine which protects it, can find a port, to call its own, within twenty thousand miles of the field of its operations. The double length of the two Americas has to be run—a stormy and tempestuous cape to be doubled—to find itself in a port of its own country: while here lies one in the very edge of its field, ours by right, ready for use, and ample for every purpose of refuge and repair, protection and domination. Can we turn our back upon it? and, in turning the back, deliver it up to the British? Insane, and suicidal would be the fatal act! . . .

Agriculturally the value of the country is great; . . .

Commercially, the advantages of Oregon will be great—far greater than any equal portion of the Atlantic States. The eastern Asiatics, who will be their chief customer, are more numerous than our customers in western Europe—more profitable to trade with, and less dangerous to quarrel with. Their articles of commerce are richer than those of Europe; they want what the Oregons will have to spare—bread and provisions—and have no systems of policy to prevent them from purchasing these necessaries of life from those who can supply them. The sea which washes their shores is every way a better sea than the Atlantic—richer in its whale and other fisheries—in the fur regions which enclose it to the north—more fortunate in the tranquillity of its character, in its freedom from storms, gulf-streams, and icebergs—in its perfect adaptation to steam navigation—in its intermediate or half-way islands, and its myriad of rich islands on its further side;—in its freedom from maritime Powers on its coasts, except the American, which is to grow up at the mouth of the Columbia. As a people to trade with—as a sea to navigate—the Mongolian race of eastern Asia, and the North Pacific ocean, are far preferable to the Europeans and the Atlantic. . . .

# God's Chosen People

The effect of the arrival of the Caucasian, or White race, on the western coast of America, opposite the eastern coast of Asia, remains to be mentioned among the benefits which the settlement of the Columbia will produce, and that a benefit, not local to us, but general and universal to the human race. Since the dispersion of man upon earth, I know of no human event, past or present, which promises a greater, and more beneficent change upon earth than the arrival of the van of the Caucasian race (the Celtic-Anglo-Saxon division) upon the border of the sea which washes the shore of the eastern Asia. The Mongolian, or Yellow race, is there, four hundred millions in number, spreading almost to Europe; a race once the foremost of the human family in the arts of civilization, but torpid and stationary for thousands of years. It is a race far above the Ethiopian, or Black—above the Malay, or Brown, (if we must admit five races)—and above the American Indian, or Red: it is a race far above all these, but still, far below the White; and like all the rest, must receive an impresion from the superior race whenever they come in contact. It would seem that the White race alone received the divine command, to subdue and replenish the earth! for it is the only race that has obeyed it—the only one that hunts out new and distant lands, and even a New World, to subdue and replenish. Starting from western Asia, taking Europe for their field, and the Sun for their guide, and leaving the Mongolians behind, they arrived, after many ages, on the shores of the Atlantic, which they lit up with the lights of science and religion, and adorned with the useful and the elegant arts. Three and a half centuries ago, this race, in obedience to the great command, arrived in the New World, and found new lands to subdue and replenish. For a long time, it was confined to the border of the new field, (I now mean the Celtic-Anglo-Saxon division;) and even fourscore years ago the philosophic [Edmund] Burke was considered a rash man because he said the English colonists would top the Alleghanies, and descend into the valley of the Mississippi, and occupy without parchment if the Crown refused to make grants of land.

What was considered a rash declaration eighty years ago, is old history, in our young country, at this day. Thirty years ago I said the same thing of the Rocky Mountains and the Columbia: it was ridiculed then: it is becoming history to-day. . . . The van of the Caucasian race now top the Rocky Mountains, and spread down to the shores of the Pacific. In a few years a great population will grow up there, luminous with the accumulated lights of European and American civilization. Their presence in such a position cannot be without its influence upon eastern Asia. The sun of civilization must shine across the sea: socially and commercially, the van of the Caucasians, and the rear of the Mongolians, must intermix. They must talk together, and trade together, and marry together. Commerce is a great civilizer—social intercourse as great—and marriage greater. The White and Yellow races can marry together, as well as eat and trade together. Moral and intellectual superiority will do the rest: the White race will take the ascendant, elevating what is susceptible of improvement—wearing out what is not. The Red race has disappeared from the Atlantic coast: the tribes that resisted civilization, met extinction. This is a cause of lamentation with many. For my part, I cannot murmur at what seems to be the effect of divine law. I cannot repine that this Capitol has replaced the wigwam—this Christian people, replaced the savages— white matrons, the red squaws—and that such men as Washington, Franklin, and Jefferson, have taken the place of Powhattan, Opechonecanough, and other red men, howsoever respectable they may have been as savages.

## White Moral and Intellectual Superiority

Civilization, or extinction, has been the fate of all people who have found themselves in the track of the advancing Whites, and civilization, always the preference of the Whites, has been pressed as an object, while extinction has followed as a consequence of its resistance. The Black and the Red races have often felt their ameliorating influence. The Yellow race, next to themselves in the scale of mental and moral excellence, and in the beauty of form, once their superiors in the useful and elegant arts, and in learning, and still respectable though stationary; this race cannot fail to receive a new impulse from the approach of the Whites, improved so much since so many ages ago they left the western borders of Asia. The apparition of the van of the Caucasian race, rising upon them in the east after having left them on the west, and after having completed the circumnavigation of the globe, must wake up and reanimate the torpid body of old Asia. Our position and policy will commend us to their hospitable reception: political considerations will aid the action of social and commercial influences. Pressed upon by the great Powers of Europe—the same that press upon us—they must in our approach see the advent of friends, not of foes—of benefactors, not of invaders. The moral and intellectual superiority of the White race will do the rest: and thus, the youngest people, and the newest land, will become the reviver and the regenerator of the oldest.

It is in this point of view, and as acting upon the social, political, and religious condition of Asia, and giving a new point of departure to her ancient civilization, that I look upon the settlement of the Columbia river by the van of the Caucasian race as the most momentous human event in the history of man since his dispersion over the face of the earth.

# Manifest Destiny Is No Justification for Aggression

*Charles Goodyear*

Many U.S. leaders of the 1840s were concerned that claims about America's Manifest Destiny were undermining the nation's relations with the rest of the world. After all, the idea that the United States had a divine right to spread throughout the New World was sure to alarm the various European powers that had interests in Canada, the Caribbean, and Central and South America. In the 1846 debate over the acquisition of Oregon territory from Great Britain, Representative Charles Goodyear rejected Manifest Destiny as a justification for angering England and possibly causing a war. He argued that Manifest Destiny was nothing but a hollow mantra used to justify the Americans' desire for more territory. Rather than expansion, Goodyear believed that the country's interests would be best served by developing the resources it already possessed.

As you read, consider the following questions:

1. In your opinion, what does Goodyear mean when he calls Manifest Destiny a "robber's title"?
2. What lesson does Goodyear feel the United States should learn from the histories of Macedonia and Rome?
3. How does Goodyear believe that the Oregon question should be settled?

---

I am aware, sir, that a claim in our favor paramount to all others has been set up—that of manifest destiny. It runs thus: God hath given to this nation the western continent

Excerpted from *Congressional Globe,* by Charles Goodyear (Washington, DC: 29th Congress, 1846).

and the fulness thereof. This, as I understand it, overrides all titles, and sets at defiance all reasoning. This claim to universal dominion was put forth in the commencement of this debate, and has been frequently urged in the course of it. . . . I regretted to hear the sentiment avowed in an American Congress, because it implies a doubt of the validity of our own perfect title, and because it has ever been used to justify every act of wholesale violence and rapine that ever disgraced the history of the world. It is the robber's title; but its record is accompanied by the instructive lesson that it ultimately meets the robber's doom.

## The Lesson of History

The Macedonian conqueror consulted the Delphic oracle, and having obtained from the priestess an equivocal answer, which, in his construction, gave him the right, by *manifest destiny,* to conquer the world, he pursued his career of victory amid sighs and tears and blood, over homes and hearths made desolate, cities wasted, and prostrate thrones, until, standing on the verge of the then habitable globe, he wept that he had not another world to conquer. Confident in the omnipotence of his fate, he drew around him his imperial robes and proudly boasted of the endless duration of his dynasty and his throne. But death struck the conqueror in a drunken revel, and his fated empire was broken into fragments, and disappeared from the earth, like the sand before the simoom of the desert. Rome, too, consulted her oracles, and sought in omens and signs her title by manifest destiny to universal empire. The response of the priest was propitious, and her legions proceeded to execute the decree. The title lost nothing of its force while there was wealth to plunder or nations to subdue; under it, the rapacity of the Roman praetor knew no bounds, his cruelty no remorse. She checked not her career of victory until the spoils of every nation, from the pillars of Hercules to the Indian ocean, swelled the triumph of her conquerors, and contributed to the luxuries and magnificence of what she fondly termed the Eternal City. "While the Colliseum stands Rome shall stand," was her proud boast. The Colliseum still stands, majestic in its ruins; but the Eternal City, long since despoiled of its glory and its power, is now only known to the traveller as the city of shattered columns and mighty recollections. The modern conqueror—the man of unbeating heart and iron nerve, who pursued his purposes with like unbending firmness upon the sands of Egypt and the snows of Russia—whose eye never quailed, and whose heart never faltered—who asserted and proved his title at that cannon's mouth, until victory, even, seemed the doomed minister of his stern and unrelenting will—he, too, pointed to his star and talked of destiny; but that bright luminary has set in perpetual night, and the eye that gazed upon its brightness was closed forever upon a barren rock in the steep Atlantic wave.

## Limit National Ambitions

Who hath read the book of fate, or fathomed the purposes of the Almighty? Sir, we may read the future by the past. I have no doubt of our destiny, if we limit our ambition to the development of the human faculties and the cultivation of the arts of peace. With a territory capable of sustaining a larger population in comfort and opulence than any other country under one Government upon earth, the human mind can scarcely limit the progress of our dominion, either in duration or extent. But if, on the other hand, we should be stimulated to territorial aggrandizement by the prospect of successful war, I have as little doubt that the western continent would soon to be found too narrow a sphere for our conquests. But with this brilliant prospect before us, we should remember that all history comes burdened with the admonition, that the nation which is destined to extend its territory by conquest, is equally fated to perish in the midst of its victories. It is due, sir, to the American people to know that their title, in this instance, needs no such equivocal alliance. In the appropriate language of the gentleman from Tennessee [Mr. Stanton] our right is our destiny, not our destiny our right. But we are led to consider, in this connexion, the duty of our Government, in case England should propose to renew the negotiation upon the basis of the division of the territory in the spirit of amicable adjustment. I answer she should be met in the same spirit; and, in case she should offer the terms recently tendered and withdrawn by this Government, they should be unhesitatingly accepted. If it was consistent with the duties of Government to make the offer then, it is proper to accept it now. The interests and rights of the two countries have in no respect changed in regard to this territory. I do not say that the negotiation should be reopened at our instance, nor that any more favorable terms should be offered or accepted. On the contrary, I think our Government, in the manifestation of its disposition to adjust this difficulty, has approached the extremest limit which the rights, the interests, or the honor of our country will warrant; and if England should prefer to try the issue of a resort to arms, we shall then be restored to our belligerent rights, and may claim and take the whole. England well knows that war is a game which more than one can play at.

## The Value of the Territory in Dispute

Sir, the inference I draw from this view of the matter is, that the notice being given, the joint occupancy terminated, and England remaining quiet, our rights to exclusive jurisdiction should be asserted only up to the 49th parallel of latitude. This being understood to be the policy and determination of our Government, the chances of war are entirely removed. England will not incur the hazards of a war for an inconsiderable tract of unproductive wilderness, the title to which she knows is clearly and unquestionably in us. This being known, the excitement upon this subject, as well in England as in this country, would entirely subside, and we should hear little more of Oregon.

But if the extreme policy, of the whole or none, urged by a few gentlemen upon this floor, is to be carried out, I cannot see how a war can be avoided. England cannot, consistently with her national honor, accept less, in the division of this territory, than has been repeatedly offered her; and, however reluctant she may be, I see not how she can escape a resort to this last dread alternative.

I proceed to consider for one moment whether it is our interest to drive her to this extremity.

Our national honor is no way concerned in the matter. By adopting the 49th parallel as our boundary we make our own terms, and dictate them, too, somewhat imperiously to the haughtiest and most powerful nation upon earth. It is, then, a mere matter of expediency, and as such I propose to consider it.

The value of the territory in dispute, compared with the expenses, the sacrifices, the sufferings, bloodshed, and horrors of a war, is the question at issue. Sir, I address not my arguments to those sublimated gentlemen who assert that the existence of a right precludes the consideration of consequences in its assertion. The gentlemen have forgotten, or haply never learned, that a regard to consequences is the first duty of a statesman; that it is that alone for which impartial history will give him credit for sagacity and wisdom.

# The Mexican War Was Both Justified and Successful

*Part I:* Democratic Review; *Part II: James K. Polk*

The editors of the *Democratic Review*, which served as a voice for the Democratic Party in the 1840s, ardently supported President Polk and the Mexican War. While the war was still under way in 1847, the *Review* published several articles blaming Mexico for the outbreak of hostilities with the United States and defending the Polk Administration's call for war. After the conclusion of the war in February 1848, Polk himself addressed Congress regarding Treaty of Guadalupe-Hidalgo, under which Mexico made vast territorial concessions to the United States. Polk emphasized the economic benefits that the new territories would provide the nation.

Excerpts from both the *Democratic Review* and Polk's July 1848 address are reprinted below. Together, they show why many Americans felt the Mexican War was necessary, justified, and ultimately beneficial to the United States.

As you read, consider the following questions:
1. Why, according to the *Democratic Review*, was the annexation of Texas not an act of war?
2. Why, in the opinion of the editors of the *Democratic Review*, should Mexico make large concessions to the United States?
3. Why, according to Polk, are the terms of the treaty with Mexico fair and just?

Part I: Excerpted from "The Mexican War—Its Origin and Conduct," *Democratic Review*, April 1847, and "The Mexican War—Its Origin, Its Justice, and Its Consequences: The Boundary of Texas Discussed," *Democratic Review,* February 1848. Part II: Excerpted from James K. Polk's speech before the United States Congress, July 6, 1848.

# I

It has been the fortune of this country, perhaps its misfortune, to have become involved in hostilities with a neighboring republic. Such a state of things was contemplated many years ago however, as possible, by our leading statesmen, to whom no intentions of precipitate action, nor any ambitious designs, were ever attributed. Indeed, we may safely aver, that if hostilities had been commenced against Mexico long before the annexation of Texas, the people of this country would have been ready to sustain such a measure, and have given it their hearty approval. . . .

## The Annexation of Texas Was Justified

The annexation of Texas is considered as one of the causes of the war, and so it has been treated both in the newspapers and on the floor of Congress. That it has to do with the war we will not deny; but if it has been made a cause of difficulty, Mexico alone is responsible for the consequences. This distinction should be kept up in the minds of all reflecting persons. The annexation of Texas was not an act of War on our part. That was a Republic which had taken its place among the nations of the earth. Its freedom was recognised officially by the most powerful of the European Governments, and diplomatic intercourse, according to the laws of nations, had grown up between Texas and its new found friends. The recognition of its independence being thus general, and fully established, left it the power to seek the alliance of France or England, or more wisely, to become a member of a confederacy, where the Ægis of liberty could be held up for its protection, and where it could affiliate with kindred interests, hopes and destinies.

Even Mexico had admitted this independent position of Texas, by a proposition and an effort to negotiate. There was no doubt then, and there can be no doubt, that the annexation of Texas was no just cause of offence to Mexico. . . .

Texas becoming an integral portion of the United States, was immediately entitled to the protection afforded to the other members of the confederacy. The boundary of the new state, as claimed by it, was recognised by the nations of the earth when they recognised its independence. Mr. Clay, however much he may have opposed the measures of the present administration, has distinctly asserted, that by the treaty of Louisiana, the boundary, as claimed by Texas, was fully established. In 1836, the Congress of Texas declared the Rio del Norte to be the boundary of the Republic; it had "exercised and extended its jurisdiction" beyond the Nueces; that portion of territory south of the Rio had been represented in the Congress of Texas; and finally, in 1845, our own Congress had included it within the circle of our revenue system, placing officers to reside there for the very purpose of supervising and sustaining it. Thus this country in each particular committed itself on this boundary question; and as the representatives of all parties in Congress assented to it, it became indisputably a settled question, "odorous with nationality."

Other measures became unavoidable, from the very nature of things, and Texas was as much entitled to our sympathy and protection, as any portion of the confederacy. That protection was needed, is a matter of history. A Mexican force threatened a fresh attack, and Texas, worn out with its long and bloody struggle for freedom, required, as it had a right to do, our prompt assistance. Thus we perceive there was an imperious necessity for action on our part; the collection of the revenue, important enough even in times of peace, to make the employment of a fleet of armed cutters indispensable, and the defence of our territory, demanded the presence of an American force in the quarter threatened. The manner in which this was done, was marked with as much judgment as delicacy.

## Mexico Initiated Hostilities

The President, through his Secretary of War, placed a small force under the command of Col. Taylor, Brevet Brigadier General, an experienced and brave officer, and by no means a senior of his grade. The propriety of this first movement is highly worthy of commendation. There was

no display of any of the pomp and circumstance of war—
no great military effort—no thrusting forward of superior
general officers, as if some grand design was intended; it
was the mere disposition of a command, in the manner
constantly practised by our Government, to protect a distant post, and as has for years been usual upon the rivers
and prairies of the far west. Still further to determine the
character of this movement, we have only to look at the instructions given by the Secretary of War to General Taylor,
which were, to abstain from all aggressive conduct towards
Mexico and the Mexicans, and to commit no act of hostility unless in self-defence. . . .

It is also evident that the whole procedure of Gen. Taylor
was in contemplation of a pacific mission. In a letter to Gen.
Worth, he declared he apprehended no collision; and that
General Worth entertained the same opinion, is evident
from his returning to the United States and desiring to
throw up his commission. Those who would charge the
Government with a desire to commence war, must, therefore shut their eyes to the instructions of the President to
Gen. Taylor, as well as to the recorded opinions of that dis-
creet officer, that there would be no collision, opinions of
which he made no secret whatever. The Mexicans took the
initiative, with their usual craftiness and love of blood. The
massacre of Col. Cross and of Lieutenant Porter, and the
unprovoked attack upon the command of Captains Thorn-
ton and Hardie, were demonstrations of hostility, worthy
only of barbarians and murderers, and these were upon territory not only known as a portion of Texas, but admitted
to be such in an official proclamation by Gen. Woll, one of
the officers of Mexico herself! The American Government
was at all times willing to treat with Mexico. It was Mexico,
unwilling to receive the olive branch, that must fairly be
charged with a premeditated design to make war. . . .

## Mexico Must Make Concessions

As to the consequences of this war, however lamentable the
loss of the many valuable lives already sacrificed, we firmly

believe the result will prove beneficial to both countries. As Mexico is responsible for the war, she must make large concessions of territory to the United States, as an indemnity for her former indebtedness and the expenses of the war, before peace can be re-established, without disgrace to the United States. This territory will be highly valuable to the United States, but was of no sort of value, but rather an embarrassment to Mexico. It will open a new field of enterprise to our ever-progressive population, and new channels of trade for the manufacturing and agricultural districts of the United States. It will cause the Mexicans to perceive the importance of doing justice to strangers, and maintaining and enforcing laws to prevent their being plundered and robbed; and, what is more important, that the Mexicans and the Spanish race are not superior to all the rest of the world. We do not believe at all in giving money to Mexico, to buy a peace. We hold that the United States have been right throughout, and are entitled, upon the principles of strict justice, to a full satisfaction from Mexico. No matter what it costs, or what sacrifices we may still be compelled to make to obtain it, this we must have, or submit to a sacrifice of our national honor. This the Mexicans fully appreciated, when they made it a *sine qua non* of peace, that they should retain the country between the Nueces and Rio Grande. They would thereby place the United States in the wrong, in the commencement of the war and the whole controversy. The United States never can and never will agree to any such thing.

[Those] who maintain that the United States have been in the wrong in the whole controversy, including the annexation of Texas, in spite of all their Christian charity and benevolence towards the poor wronged Mexicans, and their strong professions of a desire to do them full justice, still propose only to withdraw the United States forces to the east side of the Nueces, retaining all of what they call Texas to ourselves. Now, if the annexation of Texas was an aggression upon Mexico, or an unjust seizure of one of her provinces, as these good Christian statesmen contend, why do they not come up to the mark and propose, like honest men, to restore the whole of Texas. There would then be no difficulty in making a peace, for the amount which the United States would be required to pay Mexico for the expenses of the war, would raise a respectable army for the conquest of Texas.

Whatever danger there may be in blending people of different religions into one nation, where religion is established by law,—or in annexing by conquest, under arbitrary governments, which trample upon the rights of all their subjects, and conquer only to enslave,—a free nation, which shows equal toleration and protection to all religions, and conquers only to bestow freedom, has no such danger to fear. We had the same forebodings, from equally great men, in the case of the acquisition of Louisiana; but the result has belied all their predictions. Let us boldly go forward, then, in our onward march of national greatness, and fearlessly extend our boundary as far as the justice of our claims and the circumstances of war may carry them; and let our motto be—"Justice to all—humiliating concessions to none."

## II

New Mexico and Upper California have been ceded by Mexico to the United States, and now constitute a part of our country. Embracing nearly ten degrees of latitude, lying adjacent to the Oregon Territory, and extending from the Pacific Ocean to the Rio Grande, . . . it would be difficult to estimate the value of these possessions to the United States. They constitute of themselves a country large enough for a great empire, and their acquisition is second only in importance to that of Louisiana in 1803. Rich in mineral and agricultural resources, with a climate of great salubrity, they embrace the most important ports on the whole Pacific coast of the continent of North America. The possession of the ports of San Diego and Monterey and the Bay of San Francisco will enable the United States to command the already valuable and rapidly increasing commerce of the Pacific. . . . The excellent harbors of Upper California will under our flag afford security and repose to our commercial marine, and American mechanics will soon furnish ready means of shipbuilding and repair, which are now so much wanted in that distant sea. . . .

In this vast region, whose rich resources are soon to be developed by American energy and enterprise, great must be the augmentation of our commerce, and with it new and profitable demands for mechanic labor in all its branches and new and valuable markets for our manufactures and agricultural products.

While the war has been conducted with great humanity and forbearance and with complete success on our part, the peace has been concluded on terms the most liberal and magnanimous to Mexico. In her hands the territories now ceded had remained, and, it is believed, would have continued to remain, almost unoccupied, and of little value to her or to any other nation, whilst as a part of our Union they will be productive of vast benefits to the United States, to the commercial world, and the general interests of mankind.

The immediate establishment of Territorial governments and the extension of our laws over these valuable possessions are deemed to be not only important, but indispensable to preserve order and the due administration of justice within their limits, to afford protection to the inhabitants, and to facilitate the development of the vast resources and wealth which their acquisition has added to our country.

# The Mexican War Was Motivated by Greed

*Ramon Alcarez et al.*

The Mexican War began in May 1846, after a border clash between U.S. and Mexican troops near the Rio Grande. U.S. troops occupied Mexico City in September 1847, and in February 1848 the war officially ended with the signing of the Treaty of Guadalupe-Hidalgo, in which Mexico ceded to the United States nearly all the territory now included in the states of New Mexico, Utah, Nevada, Arizona, California, Texas, and western Colorado for $15 million.

Two years after the conclusion of the Mexican War, a group of Mexican writers published *The Other Side*, in which they revealed their views on the causes and nature of the war. The book was translated and widely circulated in the United States, causing many Americans to re-evaluate their justifications for the recent conflict. In the passage excerpted below, the authors charge that the Mexican War was only the latest incident in the United States' long history of using any means necessary to spread its borders across the continent.

As you read, consider the following questions:
1. What have the two expansionist goals of the United States been since its inception, according to the authors?
2. How did the United States justify its initial occupation of Mexican territory, according to the authors, and what was wrong with these claims?
3. How has this selection influenced your opinion of whether the Mexican War was justified?

Excerpted from *The Other Side: or, Notes for the History of the War Between Mexico and the United States*, by Ramon Alcarez et al., translated by Albert C. Ramsey (New York, 1850).

To explain then in a few words the true origin of the war, it is sufficient to say that the insatiable ambition of the United States, favored by our weakness, caused it. But this assertion, however veracious and well founded, requires the confirmation which we will present, along with some former transactions, to the whole world. This evidence will leave no doubt of the correctness of our impressions.

In throwing off the yoke of the mother country, the United States of the North appeared at once as a powerful nation. This was the result of their excellent elementary principles of government established while in colonial subjection. The Republic announced at its birth, that it was called upon to represent an important part in the world of Columbus. Its rapid advancement, its progressive increase, its wonderful territory, the uninterrupted augmentation of its inhabitants, and the formidable power it had gradually acquired, were many proofs of its becoming a colossus, not only for the feeble nations of Spanish America, but even for the old populations of the ancient continent.

## A Policy of Expansion

The United States did not hope for the assistance of time in their schemes of aggrandizement. From the days of their independence they adopted the project of extending their dominions, and since then, that line of policy has not deviated in the slightest degree. This conduct, nevertheless, was not perceptible to the most enlightened: but reflecting men, who examined events, were not slow in recognising it. Conde de Aranda, from whose perception the ends which the United States had resolved upon were not concealed, made use of some celebrated words. These we shall now produce as a prophecy verified by events. "This nation has been born a pigmy: in the time to come, it will be a giant, and even a colossus, very formidable in these vast regions. Its first step will be an appropriation of the Floridas to be master of the Gulf of Mexico."

The ambition of the North Americans has not been in conformity with this. They desired from the beginning to extend their dominion in such manner as to become the absolute owners of almost all this continent. In two ways they could accomplish their ruling passion: in one by bringing under their laws and authority all America to the Isthmus of Panama; in another, in opening an overland passage to the Pacific Ocean, and making good harbors to facilitate its navigation. By this plan, establishing in some way an easy communication of a few days between both oceans, no nation could compete with them. England herself might show her strength before yielding the field to her fortunate rival, and the mistress of the commercial world might for a while be delayed in touching the point of greatness to which she aspires.

In the short space of some three quarters of a century events have verified the existence of these schemes and their rapid development. The North American Republic has already absorbed territories pertaining to Great Britain, France, Spain, and Mexico. It has employed every means to accomplish this—purchase as well as usurpation, skill as well as force, and nothing has restrained it when treating of territorial acquisition. Louisiana, the Floridas, Oregon, and Texas, have successively fallen into its power. . . .

## Aggressive Acts

While the United States seemed to be animated by a sincere desire not to break the peace, their acts of hostility manifested very evidently what were their true intentions. Their ships infested our coasts; their troops continued advancing upon our territory, situated at places which under no aspect could be disputed. Thus violence and insult were united: thus at the very time they usurped part of our territory, they offered to us the hand of treachery, to have soon the audacity to say that our obstinacy and arrogance were the real causes of the war.

To explain the occupation of the Mexican territory by the troops of General Taylor, the strange idea occurred to the United States that the limits of Texas extended to the Rio Bravo del Norte. This opinion was predicated upon two distinct principles: one, that the Congress of Texas had so declared it in December, in 1836; and another, that the river mentioned had been the natural line of Louisiana. To state these reasons is equivalent at once to deciding the matter; for no one could defend such palpable absurdities. The first, which this government prizing its intelligence and civilization, supported with refined malice, would have been ridiculous in the mouth of a child. Whom could it convince that the declaration of the Texas Congress bore a legal title for the acquisition of the lands which it appropriated to itself with so little hesitation? If such a principle were recognised, we ought to be very grateful to these gentlemen senators who had the kindness to be satisfied with so little. Why not declare the limits of the rebel state extended to San Luis, to the capital, to our frontier with Guatemala?

## False Appearances

The question is so clear in itself that it would only obscure by delaying to examine it further. We pass then to the other less nonsensical than the former. In the first place to pretend that the limits of Louisiana came to the Rio Bravo, it was essential to confound this province with Texas, which never can be tolerated. . . . Again, this same province, and afterwards State of Texas, never had extended its territory to the Rio Bravo, being only to the Nueces, in which always had been established the boundary. Lastly, a large part of the territory situated on the other side of the Bravo, belonged, without dispute or doubt, to other states of the Republic—to New Mexico, Tamaulipas, Coahuila, and Chihuahua.

Then, after so many and such plain proceedings, is there one impartial man who would not consider the forcible occupation of our territory by the North American arms a shameful usurpation? Then further, this power desired to carry to the extreme the sneer and the jest. When the question had resolved itself into one of force which is the *ultima ratio* of nations as well as of kings, when it had spread desolation and despair in our populations, when many of our citizens had perished in the contest, the bloody hand of our treacherous neighbors was turned to present the olive of peace. The Secretary of State, Mr. Buchanan, on the 27th of July, 1846, proposed anew, the admission of an Envoy to open negotiations which might lead to the concluding of an honorable peace. The national government answered that it could not decide, and left it to Congress to express its opinion of the subject. Soon to follow up closely the same system of policy, they ordered a commissioner with the army, which invaded us from the east, to cause it to be understood that peace would be made when our opposition ceased. Whom did they hope to deceive with such false appearances? Does not the series of acts which we have mentioned speak louder than this hypocritical language? By that test then, as a question of justice, no one who examines it in good faith can deny our indisputable rights. Among the citizens themselves, of the nation which has made war on us, there have been many who defended the cause of the Mexican Republic. These impartial defenders have not been obscure men, but men of the highest distinction. Mexico has counted on the assistance, ineffectual, unfortunately, but generous and illustrious, of a Clay, an Adams, a Webster, a Gallatin; that is to say, on the noblest men, the most appreciated for their virtues, for their talents, and for their services. Their conduct deserves our thanks, and the authors of this work have a true pleasure in paying, in this place, the sincere homage of their gratitude.

Such are the events that abandoned us to a calamitous war; and, in the relation of which, we have endeavored not to distort even a line of the private data consulted, to prove, on every occasion, all and each of our assertions.

From the acts referred to, it has been demonstrated to the very senses, that the real and effective cause of this war that afflicted us was the spirit of aggrandizement of the United States of the North, availing itself of its power to conquer us. Impartial history will some day illustrate for ever the conduct observed by this Republic against all laws, divine and human, in an age that is called one of light, and which is, notwithstanding, the same as the former—one of *force and violence.*

# The Republic Shall Encompass All of the Americas

*Orestes A. Brownson*

America's westward expansion did not end with the acquisition of Texas, Oregon, and California. The federal government purchased Alaska from Russia in 1867, and the expansionist impulse did not truly fade until after the close of the nineteenth century, when the United States acquired Hawaii, Guam, Puerto Rico, and (briefly) the Philippines. However, expansionist ambitions were at their greatest in the decades following the Mexican War. The following selection reveals just how far some Americans hoped Manifest Destiny would extend. It is excerpted from Orestes A. Brownson's 1865 book *The American Republic*. Brownson, a social philosopher, author, and clergyman, predicts that the United States will eventually span all of North and South America.

As you read, consider the following questions:
1. What is the United States' divine mission, according to Brownson?
2. What is the author's opinion of expansion through violent conquest?
3. How does Brownson believe that the annexation of Canada and Mexico will be accomplished?

---

The Jews were the chosen people of God, through whom the primitive traditions were to be preserved in their purity

Excerpted from *The American Republic*, by Orestes A. Brownson (New York: P. O'Shea, 1865).

and integrity, and the Messiah was to come. The Greeks were the chosen people of God, for the development and realization of the beautiful or the divine splendor in art, and of the true in science and philosophy; and the Romans, for the development of the state, law, and jurisprudence. The great despotic nations of Asia were never properly nations; or if they were nations with a mission, they proved false to it, and count for nothing in the progressive development of the human race. History has not recorded their mission, and as far as they are known they have contributed only to the abnormal development or corruption of religion and civilization. Despotism is barbaric and abnormal.

## America's Unique Contribution to Civilization

The United States, or the American Republic, has a mission, and is chosen of God for the realization of a great idea. It has been chosen not only to continue the work assigned to Greece and Rome, but to accomplish a greater work than was assigned to either. In art, it will prove false to its mission if it do not rival Greece; and in science and philosophy, if it do not surpass it. In the state, in law, in jurisprudence, it must continue and surpass Rome. Its idea is liberty, indeed, but liberty with law, and law with liberty. Yet its mission is not so much the realization of liberty as the realization of the true idea of the state, which secures at once the authority of the public and the freedom of the individual—the sovereignty of the people without social despotism, and individual freedom without anarchy. In other words, its mission is to bring out in its life the dialectic union of authority and liberty, of the natural rights of man and those of society. . . .

Of all the states or colonies on this continent, the American Republic alone has a destiny, or the ability to add any thing to the civilization of the race. Canada and the other British Provinces, Mexico and Central America, Columbia and Brazil, and the rest of the South American States, might be absorbed in the United States without being missed by the civilized world. They represent no idea, and the work of civilization could go on without them as well as with them. If they keep up with the progress of civilization, it is all that can be expected of them. France, England, Germany, and Italy might absorb the rest of Europe, and all Asia and Africa, without withdrawing a single laborer from the work of advancing the civilization of the race; and it is doubtful if these nations themselves can severally or jointly advance it much beyond the point reached by the Roman Empire, except in abolishing slavery and including in the political people the whole territorial people. They can only develop and give a general application to the fundamental principles of the Roman constitution. That indeed is much, but it adds no new element nor new combination of pre-existing elements. But nothing of this can be said of the United States. . . .

Count de Maistre predicted early in the century the failure of the United States, because they have no proper name; but his prediction assumed what is not the fact. The United States have a proper name by which all the world knows and calls them. The proper name of the country is America: that of the people is Americans. Speak of Americans simply, and nobody understands you to mean the people of Canada, Mexico, Brazil, Peru, Chile, Paraguay, but everybody understands you to mean the people of the United States. The fact is significant, and foretells for the people of the United States a continental destiny, as is also foreshadowed in the so-called "Monroe doctrine," which France, during our domestic troubles, was permitted, on condition of not intervening in our civil war in favor of the rebellion, to violate.

## Peaceful Annexation

There was no statesmanship in proclaiming the "Monroe doctrine," for the statesman keeps always, as far as possible, his government free to act according to the exigencies of the case when it comes up, unembarrassed by previous declarations of principles. Yet the doctrine only expresses the destiny of the American people, and which nothing but their own fault can prevent them from realizing in its own good time. Napoleon will not succeed in his Mexican policy, and Mexico will add some fifteen or twenty new States to the American Union as soon as it is clearly for the interests of all parties that it should be done, and it can be done by mutual consent, without war or violence. The Union will fight to maintain the integrity of her domain and the supremacy of her laws within it, but she can never, consistently with her principles or her interests, enter upon a career of war and conquest. Her system is violated, endangered, not extended, by subjugating her neighbors, for subjugation and liberty go not together. Annexation, when it takes place, must be on terms of perfect equality, and by the free act of the state annexed. The Union can admit of no inequality of rights and franchises between the States of which it is composed. The Canadian Provinces and the Mexican and Central American States, when annexed, must be as free as the original States of the Union, sharing alike in the power and the protection of the Republic—alike in its authority, its freedom, its grandeur, and its glory, as one free, independent, self-governing people. They may gain much, but must lose nothing by annexation. . . . The American people need not trouble themselves about their exterior expansion. That will come of itself as fast as desirable.

# 4

# THE WESTERN RAILROADS

# CHAPTER PREFACE

The closing of the American frontier began on May 10, 1869, when the golden spike was driven at a ceremony in Promontory, Utah, marking the completion of the nation's first transcontinental railroad. Plans for such a road had their origins in the 1840s, when "Oregon fever" and the doctrine of Manifest Destiny first swept the nation. However, disagreements between northerners and southerners about what the railroad's eastern terminus should be kept Congress from funding the project. Only after the outbreak of the Civil War was Congress able to pass the Pacific Railroad Act of 1862. This act chartered the Union Pacific Railroad to be built westward from Omaha and for the Central Pacific Railroad to be built eastward from San Francisco. Other transcontinental railroads followed, including the Santa Fe line that stretched to Los Angeles and the Northern Pacific that reached to Puget Sound.

The impact of the western railroads was extraordinary. They increased western immigration and settlement, stimulated the development of mining and other industries, and led to the rise of western cities such as Los Angeles, Denver, and Omaha. The railroads gave rise to one of the institutions most associated with the so-called Wild West: the long drive, in which cowboys drove herds of cattle from Texas up to Kansas rail stations for transport east. The railroads made the profitable cattle drives possible, but during the 1880s they also helped bring an end to open range as they encouraged thousands of farmers to settle the plains. Throughout the 1870s and 1880s the railroads accelerated the American farmer's century-old practice of heading west in search of unclaimed or inexpensive land on the western frontier.

By 1890 all of the western territories except Oklahoma, New Mexico, and Arizona had achieved statehood. With the settlement of the western frontier, America's westward expansion was almost complete.

# The United States Should Build a Transcontinental Railroad

*William Gilpin*

William Gilpin had made his living as a lieutenant in the Seminole War, a newspaper editor, and a lawyer before heading to Oregon to promote and organize settlement in 1843. He later served in the Mexican War and was appointed governor of the Colorado Territory. In 1859 he wrote a book called *The Central Gold Region* in which he argued that Colorado would become the center of world civilization and commerce. Part of his vision was that Denver would be the center of a network of railroads connecting all of the United States. This vision was not entirely accurate, but Gilpin's insights into the benefits of a transcontinental railroad were. He knew that a transcontinental railroad would do what Thomas Jefferson had originally hoped a "Northwest Passage" would—greatly stimulate trade across the Pacific Ocean. The following excerpts from Gilpin's book are reprints of a speech he gave in Independence, Missouri, in 1849.

As you read, consider the following questions:
1. Are there overtones of Manifest Destiny in Gilpin's remarks? Cite specific examples from the text.
2. What effect will a transcontinental railroad have on the economies of the East Coast, in Gilpin's view?

Excerpted from *The Central Gold Region: The Grain, Pastoral, and Gold Regions of North America with Some New Views of Its Physical Geography; and Observations on the Pacific Railroad*, by William Gilpin (Philadelphia: Sower, Barnes & Co., 1860).

Diplomacy and war have brought to us the completion of our territory and peace. From this we advance to the RESULTS. These results are, for the present, the imperial expansion of our Republic to the other ocean, fraternity with Asia, and the construction across the centre of our territory, from ocean to ocean, of a great iron pathway, specially national to us, international to the northern continents of America, Asia, and Europe. . . .

## U.S. Expansion

Up to the year 1840, the progress whereby twenty-six States and four Territories had been established and peopled, had amounted to a solid strip of twenty-five miles in depth, added annually, along the western face of the Union from Canada to the Gulf. This occupation of wild territory, accumulating outward like the annual rings of our forest trees, proceeds with all the solemnity of a Providential ordinance. It is at this moment sweeping onward to the Pacific with accelerated activity and force, like a deluge of men, rising unabatedly, and daily pushed onward by the hand of God. . . .

From this very spot [Independence] had gone forth a forlorn hope to occupy Oregon and California; Texas was thus annexed, the Indian country pressed upon its flanks, and spy companies reconnoitering New and Old Mexico. . . . Thus, then, *overland* sweeps this tide-wave of population, absorbing in its thundering march the glebe, the savages, and the wild beasts of the wilderness, sealing the mountains and debouching down upon the seaboard. Upon the high Atlantic sea-coast, the pioneer force has thrown itself into ships, and found in the ocean-fisheries food for its creative genius. The whaling fleet is the *marine* force of the pioneer army. These two forces, by land and sea, have worked steadily onward to the North Pacific. They now reunite in the harbors of Oregon and California, about to bring into existence upon the Pacific a commercial grandeur identical with that which has followed them upon the Atlantic. . . .

To the American people, then, belongs this vast interior space, covered over its uniform surface of 2,300,000 square miles, with the richest calcareous soil, touching the snows towards the north, and the torrid heats towards the south, bound together by an infinite internal navigation, of a temperate climate, and constituting, in the whole, the most magnificent dwelling-place marked out by God for man's abode. As the complete beneficence of the Almighty has thus given to us, the owners of the continent, the great natural outlets of the Mississippi to the Gulf, and the St. Lawrence to the North Atlantic, so is it left to a pious and grateful people, appreciating this goodness, to construct through the gorge of the Sierra Madre [Rockies], a great artificial monument, an iron path, a NATIONAL Railway to the *Western* Sea. . . .

## A Broad Road of Commerce

The experience gained from the great works constructed by the last generation in digging through the Alleghenies routes for commerce to the Atlantic, settles for us the rules that shall guide *us* across the Sierra Madre [Rockies] to the Pacific. In 1818 the State of New York cut through the low and narrow ridge between Rome and Syracuse, the former on an affluent of the Hudson, the latter of Lake Ontario. Thus the *first* expenditures, perforating the dividing mountain, let through that infant commerce, which in thirty years has grown to such a grandeur of quantity and profit, that this great thoroughfare is itself quadrupled in capacity and lengthened out to Montreal, to Boston, to New York City and into Pennsylvania, towards the east. Westward, it reaches through Ohio and Indiana to the Ohio river, and by the Illinois and Wisconsin rivers to the Missouri and Mississippi. What the single State of New York, of 1,200,000 population, accomplished by her own intrinsic bravery and resources, undismayed by ridicule and unappalled by the *then* experimental character of such works in a republic and upon our continent:—just such a work now invites the national bravery, power, and wealth of this imperial republic;

namely to lay, over the dividing barrier of the Sierra Madre, along the floor of its natural tunnel at the South Pass, *an iron pathway,* which, descending the grades of the Platte and Columbia to the highest points of navigation, shall let through the first infant stream of that supreme Oriental commerce, whose annually expanding flood will, during our generation, elongate its arms and fingers through all the States and to every harbor of the two seaboards. . . .

It is, then, I repeat, through the heart of our Territories, our population, our States, our farms and habitations, that we need this broad current of commerce. Where passengers and cargo may, at any time or place, embark upon or leave the vehicles of transportation. . . . This central railroad is an essential domestic institution, more powerful and permanent than law, or popular consent, to thoroughly complete the great systems of fluvial arteries which fraternize us into one people; to bind the two seaboards to this one nation, like ears to the human head; to radicate the foundations of the UNION so broad and deep, and render its structure so solid, that no possible force or stratagem can shake its permanence; and to secure such scope and space to progress, that prosperity and equality shall never be impaired or chafe for want of room.

## Rich Trade with the Orient

What, sirs, are these populous empires of Japan and China, now become our neighbors? They are the most ancient, the most highly civilized, the most polished of the earth. It was from Sinim [China] that the Judean king Solomon imported the architects, the mechanics, the furniture of his gorgeous temple. . . . Hence came the climax of all human inventions, *letters and figures,* which fix language and numbers, making them eternal. . . . Tea, sugar, the peach produced from the wild almond, the orange from the sour lime, the apple from the crab, the fruits, the flowers, the vegetables of our gardens, are the *creations* of Chinese *horticultural* science. The horse, cattle, the swine and poultry of our farms, come to us from thence. . . . Hence also came gunpowder, the magnetic needle, and calomel. The paints, varnish, and tools of the art have come, and the remedies used in pharmacy.

Such as *Progress* is to-day, the same has it been for ten thousand years. It is the stream of the human race flowing from the east to the west, impelled by the same divine instinct that pervades creation. . . .

It is by the rapid propagation of new States, the immediate occupation of the broad platform of the continent, the aggregation of the Pacific Ocean and Asiatic commerce, that inquietude will be swallowed up, and the murmurs of discontent lost in the onward sound of advancement. Discontent, distanced, will die out. The immense wants of the Pacific will draw off, over the Western outlets, the over-teeming crops of the Mississippi Valley. Thus will the present seaboard States resume again their once profitable monopoly of the European market, relieved from the competition of the interior States. The cotton and rice culture of Georgia and the Carolinas will revive. The tobacco of Virginia and Maryland will again alone reach Europe. Ships withdrawn from the Northern States to the Pacific, will regenerate the noble business of nautical construction in New England and New York. The established domestic manufactures of clothing and metals will find, in our great home extension, that protection which they in vain seek to create by unequal legislation, nocuous and impracticable in our present incomplete and unbalanced geographical form. Thus calmly weighed and liberally appreciated, does this great Central Railroad minister to the interests, and invite the advocacy and co-operation of every section of our territory, and every citizen of our common country.

# The Transcontinental Railroad Is a Great Achievement

*Philadelphia* Bulletin

Construction of a transcontinental railroad began in earnest with the Pacific Railroad Act of 1862, which chartered the Union Pacific Railroad to be built westward from Omaha and for the Central Pacific Railroad to be built eastward from San Francisco. The two lines were joined at Promontory, Utah, in May 1869, an event that was greeted with nationwide celebrations. In the late 1860s, even before it was completed, many Americans viewed the transcontinental railroad as a perfect symbol of American economic and technological progress. This view is evident in the Philadelphia *Bulletin*'s 1868 description of the building of the Union Pacific.

As you read, consider the following questions:
1. How does the author liken the process of railroad construction to a military operation?
2. What optimistic terms does the author use to describe the building of the transcontinental railroad?

---

One can see all along the line of the now completed road the evidences of ingenious self-protection and defence which our men learned during the war. The same curious huts and underground dwellings which were a common sight along our army lines then, may now be seen burrowed into the sides of the hills, or built up with ready

Excerpted from *Progress of the Union Pacific West from Omaha, Nebraska, Across the Continent*, by the Philadelphia *Bulletin*, edited by Union Pacific Railroad Company (New York: Union Pacific Railroad Company, 1868).

adaptability in sheltered spots. The whole organisation of the force engaged in the construction of the road is, in fact, semi-military. The men who go ahead, locating the road, are the advance guard. Following these is the second line, cutting through the gorges, grading the road, and building bridges. Then comes the main line of the army, placing the sleepers, laying the track, spiking down the rails, perfecting the alignment, ballasting the rail, and dressing up and completing the road for immediate use. This army of workers has its base, to continue the figure, at Omaha, Chicago, and still farther eastward, from whose markets are collected the material for constructing the road. Along the line of the completed road are construction trains constantly "pushing forward to the front" with supplies. The company's grounds and workshops at Omaha are the arsenal, where these purchases, amounting now to millions of dollars in value, are collected and held ready to be sent forward. . . . The advanced limit of the rail is occupied by a train of long box cars, with hammocks swung under them, beds, spread on top of them, bunks built within them, in which the sturdy, broad-shouldered pioneers of the great iron highway sleep at night, and take their meals. Close behind this train come loads of ties and rails and spikes, &c., which are being thundered off upon the roadside to be ready for the track-layers. The road is graded a hundred miles in advance. The ties are laid roughly in place, then adjusted, gauged and leveled. Then the track is laid.

Track-laying on the Union Pacific is a science, and we, pundits of the Far East, stood upon that embankment, only about a thousand miles this side of sunset, and backed westward before that hurrying corpos of sturdy operators with a mingled feeling of amusement, curiosity and profound respect. On they came. A light car, drawn by a single horse, gallops up to the front with its load of rails. Two men seize the end of a rail and start forward, the rest of the gang taking hold by twos, untill it is clear of the car. They come forward at a run. At the word of command the rail is dropped in its place, right side up with care, while the same process goes on at the other side of the car. Less than thirty seconds to a rail for each gang, and so four rails go down to the minute! Quick work, you say, but the fellows on the U.P. are tremendously in earnest. The moment the car is empty it is tipped over on the side of the track to let the next loaded car pass it, and then it is tipped back again, and it is a sight to see it go flying back for another load, propelled by a horse at full gallop at the end of sixty or eighty feet of rope, ridden by a young Jehu, who drives furiously. Close behind the first gang come the gaugers, spikers and bolters, and a lively time they make of it. It is a grand Anvil Chorus that those sturdy sledges are playing across the plains. It is in a triple time, three strokes to the spike. There are ten spikes to a rail, four hundred rails to a mile, eighteen hundred miles to San Francisco. That's the sum, what is the quotient? Twenty-one million times are those sledges to be swung—twenty-one million times are they to come down with their sharp punctuation, before the great work of modern America is complete! On they go. Fifteen minutes from the moment that the rail is dropped upon the track, it is adjusted, spiked, bolted to its predecessor with the "fish-plate," (there are no "chairs" used) and ready for the advancing train. It was worth the dust, the heat, the cinders, the hurrying ride, day and night, the fatigue and the exposure, to see with one's own eyes this second grand "March to the Sea." [Union general William Tecumseh] Sherman, with his victorious legions, sweeping from Atlanta to Savannah, was a spectacle less glorious than this army of men, marching on foot from Omaha to Sacramento, subduing unknown wilderness, scaling unknown mountains, surmounting untried obstacles and binding across the broad breast of America the iron emblem of modern progress and civilization.

# Working on the Railroad

*Edward Pierce Coleman*

Railroads brought rapid settlement and development to isolated western territories such as Idaho. Before the western railroads could be built, however, railroad survey crews had to scout out potential routes through vast frontier regions. Edward Pierce Coleman, an engineer who helped survey the route for the Oregon Short Line through Idaho, an early offshoot of the Union Pacific, encountered deserts, gorges, snowstorms, and swamps, as well as Indians and outlaws, in the course of surveys he conducted from 1881 to 1884. In the following excerpts from his memoirs, Coleman paints a colorful portrait of the western frontier.

As you read, consider the following questions:
1. Why was Coleman glad to have ridden on the stagecoach line from Walla Walla, Washington, to Boise, Idaho?
2. What were some of the hardships involved in railroad surveying, as described by the author?
3. What is the author's opinion of the Chinese who helped build the western railroads?

---

It was a hard trip from Lewiston to Boise in those days. We took the steamer down the Snake to Texas Ferry. The next morning, by a little narrow gauge railroad, we reached Walla Walla at noon. The Oregon Railway and Navigation Company were building from Walla Walla to Pendleton but were only a few miles out of Walla Walla. All that night we drove through the Blue Mountains reaching La Grande the next morning.

There was a timber fire in the mountains. It was on both

Excerpted from *Steel Rails and Territorial Tales: Forty Months Building the Oregon Short Line Railroad Through Idaho*, by Edward Pierce Coleman, edited by Philip Sinclair Nicholson (Boise, ID: Limberlost Press, 1994).

sides of the stage road and I found it uncomfortably warm riding on top of the coach. It was a grand sight. The six horses, all excited by the fire, dashed along. The driver, with his foot on the brake, and keeping his leader team taut, took the curves and grades on the run. These stage drivers were experts in their line.

## The Last of the Stagecoach Lines
This stage line from Walla Walla to Boise and on to Kelton, Utah, was said to be the longest stage road in the United States. They had a schedule to make just as trains do today. Seldom was there an accident and each driver did his best to be on time.

It was a real job to handle six spirited horses attached to a big Concord Coach, often carrying twelve to sixteen passengers, with the stage boots full of baggage, express, and mail. The coach ahead of us had been held up by a highwayman, so we had a guard armed with two big sixshooters and a sawed-off double-barrel shotgun loaded with buck shot. We, however, were not held up.

The days were hot and the nights cold enough to freeze water. The dust was something awful, especially the last day of the trip. We reached Baker City for supper and that night drove through Burnt River Canyon, reaching Huntington for breakfast. We crossed Snake River into Idaho at Olds Ferry and reached Middleton, on the Boise River, for supper and Boise City after midnight.

Seventy-two hours without any sleep! We were wrecks. We wanted to stop off over night at Baker City but were advised that because of a gold strike in the Sawtooth Mountains, which had started a stampede there and filling every stage, we might have to wait several days for a coach which could pick us up. So we hung to that coach.

The clerk at the Overland Hotel in Boise registered us and, giving each a lighted candle, showed us our rooms. I set my candlestick down on the table and headed for the bed. That is the last I remember. That evening they found me stretched across the bed just as I came in: cap, overcoat and boots all on. They aroused me and I got up, washed and went down to supper, then back to bed when I undressed and had a splendid night's rest and caught up on my sleep. I don't think the trip really injured me, but our topographer, a German and very heavy, I believe never fully recovered from the effects from that long, hard and dusty ride from Walla Walla, Washington, to Boise, Idaho, 300 miles. It was the hardest trip I ever took, but I would not have missed the experience for a good deal.

That was the last long stage line, but it was just like the old overland lines reaching from the Missouri to the Pacific twenty years earlier but operating the same. The driver's division was fifty miles long. He drove six horses which were changed every ten or twelve miles. The road was over mountains, through deserts, along dugways, often hundreds of feet above the bottom of the canyon. Another year this stage line was a thing of the past. So I am glad I had my ride on it.

## The Novelty of Electric Light

At Boise City, two parties were being organized; one to run a line into the Yellowstone and the other to run a line up the North Platte from Fort Laramie to Fort Steele. Our party was the second one. We took the train on the Oregon Short Line at Kuna and went back over the road we had been helping to build during the last two years. We changed to Union Pacific at Granger, Wyoming, reaching Cheyenne just before midnight. Here I saw my first electric lights. Cheyenne had just installed an arc light system and the kids had not gotten over the novelty of it and I saw them playing marbles in the street at midnight.

We outfitted at Cheyenne, having two, four-mule teams to transport our outfit and pulled out for Fort Laramie one hundred miles north on the North Platte. . . .

## The Ranchers' Frontier

I have never seen such large prairie dog towns as some we travelled through, miles in extent. At the Searight ranch, on the Poison Spider Creek, we saw mounds formed by the seepage of crude oil. We dug up some of the springy substance of which the mounds were composed and found it burned readily. That was before oil was discovered in Wyoming. Some of the boys proposed coming back and filing on some of this land, but I don't think they ever did.

The whole country was held by a lot of big ranch companies, and they ran off anyone who tried to file on land within their fences. Some of these companies had miles and miles of fence enclosing thousands of acres of government land and running as many as 100,000 head of cattle. Between Cheyenne and Fort Laramie, we travelled along a four-wire fence for thirty miles without a break in it and woe to the man who should cut it.

Our good weather deserted us in December, and we had snow storms and sub-zero weather. The day before Christmas, we made camp on the Sweetwater near Tom Sun's ranch. Early Christmas morning a blizzard tore our tents to pieces. We got further down in our sleeping bags and waited for day. As soon as it was light we loaded our outfit and struck out for Rawlins. The snow had ceased but the wind was so heavy that the teams could hardly make headway against it. We were all day going thirteen miles. Our Christmas dinner consisted of frozen soda biscuits and bacon. . . .

## A Harsh Winter

It was about the first of February before we were in the field, and even then the snow was so deep we made little headway. Our job was to run a line through Bear River Canyon to cut out the Colliston hill on the Utah Northern. Fortunately, the spring broke early for that country. We struggled along through deep snow and sub-zero weather all of February and March, and how we did long for spring. In the latter part of March, the weather broke, the snow melted, and as though by magic, the country was full of meadowlarks. 1 never experienced such a delightful change. Soon the trees were in leaf and the entire landscape was bright with bloom. We had had such a terrible two months that we were all set to enjoy the change.

While the snow meld rapidly, until it was gone the glare of the sun on the snow burned our faces to a crisp. We had to wear colored glasses to keep from getting snowblind, and to protect our faces, we wore green veils with an opening about three-by-five inches in front of our glasses. This opening was bound with leather to make it stay open so one could see out. We were a queer looking outfit. One day about noon, we went up a gulch leading up to the little town of Weston. The school house was on the side of this gulch and the children were coasting below the school house. When they saw us, they set up an awful howling and rushed yelling for the school house. The teacher, hearing the noise, came to the door, gave us a wild look, pulled the kids inside and slammed the door. We wondered what all the excitement was about and did not discover until we reached the store and told the merchant. He laughed and said, "If you only knew how you look to a stranger, you would not wonder that the kids and teacher were frightened."

It was in Bear River Canyon that we saw a real avalanche from its very beginning. A chunk of snow, dropped from a ledge way up toward the top of the mountain, formed a big ball which rolled down the slope until its weight started a slide which tore down the mountainside taking everything in its path and finally leaped over the cliff on the edge of Bear River breaking the ice which was a foot or more thick, and for a while, formed quite a dam in the river. None of us happened to be in the path of this avalanche.

Our line ran through the Arimo swamps and ended at Pocatello. The Arimo swamps were great tule beds forming a mat strong enough to hold a man up if he moved cautiously. Under this mat was water and mud twenty feet deep. We took soundings every hundred feet, often finding no bottom. It was hot in the tules, which were way above our heads, and the mosquitoes were a fright. Several of the boys were subjects for the hospital before we completed the work. . . .

# The Vastness of the Plains

We were shipped up to Granger, Wyoming, and several new members right from the East were added to our party. These boys had never seen mountains before and had no idea how deceptive distances were in the mountain countries. Shortly after joining us, they decided they would like to go fishing. They could see the Unita mountains southwest of us and thought they could go over there and back in a day by starting early and have time to do some fishing. These mountains were some eighty or ninety miles away, but to them, they looked to be possibly ten miles away.

They left camp Sunday morning about 3:30. The cook put them up a good lunch, but no one in camp told them anything. We thought they would learn for themselves. Mr. Clark happened to be away but returned in the afternoon. When he learned what we had done, he said we would have to keep a beacon fire burning on the hill nearby so that the boys would be able to find camp when it was dark. We cut a great pile of sage and, as soon as it was dark, lighted a fire which we took turns keeping up. About midnight, the fishers returned. They said they never would have found camp, but for the fire. They had travelled towards the mountains until long in the afternoon, and as the mountains seemed to be as far away as ever, they turned and headed for camp after eating the lunch and drinking what water one of them had been wise enough to take with him. They had a lesson in deceptive distances in the mountains. They were footsore and weary, but appreciated the story one of our camp told them of the man who had been travelling for hours toward a mountain which was still no nearer, when coming to a irrigating ditch a few feet wide, began to take off his clothing saying he was not taking any chances as that ditch was likely to run a half-mile wide.

We reran the alignment of the Oregon Short Line from Granger to Soda Springs. The railway follows Ham's Fork of the Green River which we found was full of mountain trout. . . .

# Chinese Workers

Much depends on the kind of a cook the camp has as to the life in any party. With a cook who supplies plenty of well-cooked food at the regular time the life of the party runs along as smooth as oil. With a cook who does not cook well, or takes no interest in his work, and does not care for variety in his menu, the meals become monotonous and the very life of the camp is disrupted. . . .

We had one Chinese cook for a little while who was pretty well up in English. He read American newspapers; he spoke good English and the last I heard of him, he was acting as interpreter in one of the seaports. One of our cooks argued with one of our boys that a good spirit would not hurt one; therefore, keep on the good side of the bad spirit to keep him from hurting you.

All of these Chinamen were shipped into this country by Chinese companies (Tongs) whose business it was to see that each Chinaman they brought over got back to China, either alive, or his bones were to be shipped back if he died here. This his government required. Each Chinaman hoped to save enough money while here to be able to go back to China and live in affluence; but, as they are all natural gamblers, the majority left their savings in the Fan Tan or other games they loved to play.

When Henry (Au Toy), came to us, I happened to have a set of chop sticks I had bought as a curio. When I showed them to Henry, he said, "You sabe?" I said, "No, I don't know how to use them." He showed me the right and wrong way to hold them. Told me how his father and mother punished him for holding them the wrong way. I soon got so I could eat with them to his satisfaction. I found use for this knowledge when I went to look for him when he was lost.

I have had a good deal of experience with Chinamen in Montana, Utah, Idaho and California and I always found them trustworthy. The fruit growers in California always said that a Chinaman's word was as good as his bond. When one agreed to do anything, he would fulfill the agreement even at a loss. Many of the American families in California had Chinese servants who had been with them for many years and were like one of the family.

## End of an Adventure

After completing the work to Soda Springs, we were shipped back to Valley, Nebraska, and reran the railroad line from there to Marysville, Kansas. While at Valley, the national election was held. I was a great admirer of James G. Blame and tried to talk the election board into letting me vote, but to no purpose. I was a man without a residence, so I lost my first Presidential vote.

We were given a tourist sleeper in which we lived while on this job, buying our meals along the road anywhere we could arrange it. When we reached Marysville, Kansas, we were disbanded and shipped back to Omaha. . . .

The greatest thing I got out of my experience in the engineer department was health. When I joined the party, I was under weight, very thin, of an unhealthy color and a poor sleeper. I came out of the party of good weight, tanned like an Indian, and as tough as a pine knot. I had captured health which has been with me ever since.

# The Railroads Contribute to the Destruction of the Buffalo

*William E. Webb*

Railroads transformed the western plains in a variety of ways. They certainly hastened the destruction of the vast buffalo herds that once roamed the plains, and in doing so, put an end to many Plains Indians' traditional way of life. Railroad construction crews killed buffalo for food, and the white hunters who arrived on the trains killed hundreds of buffalo for sport or to obtain their valuable hides, often shooting from railcar windows. Because the buffalo did not run from the sound of gunfire, it was possible for a single hunter to kill dozens of the animals in a matter of hours, and more than a hundred in a single day. The following account is from William E. Webb, a writer who witnessed such slaughter during his travels west.

As you read, consider the following questions:
1. How do the buffalo respond to oncoming trains, according to Webb?
2. Does the author disapprove of the buffalo hunters?
3. What does Webb predict will happen if the slaughter of the buffalo continues?

During certain periods in the spring and fall, when the large herds are crossing the Kansas Pacific Railroad, the trains run for a hundred miles or more among countless thousands of the shaggy monarchs of the plains. The bison has a

Excerpted from *Buffalo Land: An Authentic Narrative of the Adventures and Misadventures of a Late Scientific and Sporting Party upon the Great Plains of the West*, by William E. Webb (Chicago: E. Hannaford, 1872).

strange and entirely unaccountable instinct or habit which leads it to attempt crossing in front of any moving object near it. It frequently happened, in the time of the old stages, that the driver had to rein up his horses until the herd which he had startled had crossed the road ahead of him. . . .

When the iron-horse comes rushing into their solitudes, and snorting out his fierce alarms, the herds, though perhaps a mile away from his path, will lift their heads and gaze intently for a few moments toward the object thus approaching them with a roar which causes the earth to tremble, and enveloped in a white cloud that streams further and higher than the dust of the old stage-coach ever did; and then, having determined its course, instead of fleeing back to the distant valleys, away they go, charging across the ridge over which the iron rails lie, apparently determined to cross in front of the locomotive at all hazards. The rate per mile of passenger trains is slow upon the plains, and hence it often happens that the cars and buffalo will be side by side for a mile or two, the brutes abandoning the effort to cross only when their foe has merged entirely ahead. During these races the car-windows are opened, and numerous breech-loaders fling hundreds of bullets among the densely crowded and flying masses. Many of the poor animals fall, and more go off to die in the ravines. The train speeds on, and the scene is repeated every few miles until Buffalo Land is passed. . . .

Let this slaughter continue for ten years, and the bison of the American continent will become extinct. The number of valuable robes and pounds of meat which would thus be lost to us and posterity, will run too far into the millions to be easily calculated. All over the plains, lying in disgusting masses of putrefaction along valley and hill, are strewn immense carcasses of wantonly slain buffalo. They line the Kansas Pacific Railroad for two hundred miles.

# The Railroads Gave Birth to "Cow Towns"

*Joseph G. McCoy*

The railroads gave rise to a new phase of western development around 1867, when the Kansas Pacific Railroad reached Abilene, Kansas, and "cattle kings" in Texas began employing cowboys to drive their herds up the Chisholm Trail or the Goodnight-Loving Trail to towns like Abilene. At Abilene, the cattle could be shipped to markets in the East, which was experiencing an acute beef shortage as a result of the Civil War. The rise of Abilene and other "cow towns" in the late 1860s marked the beginning of the cattle driving era. Illinois meat dealer Joseph G. McCoy described the rise of Abilene as a cattle market in his 1874 book *Historic Sketches of the Cattle Trade of the West and Southwest*.

As you read, consider the following questions:
1. Why was Abilene selected as the destination of the first cattle drives, according to McCoy?
2. How was word of Abilene initially spread, as described by McCoy?
3. What hardships characterized the first cattle drives to Abilene?

---

After spending a few days investigating, Abilene, then as now, the county seat of Dickinson county, was selected as the point of location for the coming enterprise. Abilene in 1867 was a very small, dead place, consisting of about one dozen log huts, low, small, rude affairs, four-fifths of which were covered with dirt for roofing; indeed, but one shingle roof

Excerpted from *Historic Sketches of the Cattle Trade of the West and Southwest*, by Joseph G. McCoy (Kansas City, MO: Ramsey, Millett, and Hudson, 1874).

could be seen in the whole city. The business of the burg was conducted in two small rooms, mere log huts, and of course the inevitable saloon also in a log hut, was to be found.

The proprietor of the saloon was a corpulent, jolly, good-souled, congenial old man of the backwoods pattern, who, in his younger days, loved to fish and hunt, and enjoyed the life of the frontiersman. For his amusement a colony of pet prairie dogs were located on his lots, and often the old gentleman might be seen feeding his pets. Tourists and others often purchased one or more of these dogs, and took them East as curiosities. . . .

A tract of land adjoining the town was purchased for the location of the stock yards, hotel, offices, etc.

## A Choice Location

Abilene was selected because the country was entirely unsettled, well watered, excellent grass, and nearly the entire area of country was adapted to holding cattle. And it was the farthest point east at which a good depot for cattle business could have been made. Although its selection was made by an entire stranger to the country adjoining, and upon his practical judgment only, time has proved that no other so good point can be found in the State for the cattle trade. The advantages and requirements were all in its favor. After the point had been decided upon, the labor of getting material upon the ground began.

From Hannibal, Missouri, came the pine lumber, and from Lenape, Kansas, came the hard wood, and work began in earnest and with energy. In sixty days from July 1st a shipping yard, that would accommodate three thousand cattle, a large pair of Fairbank's scales, a barn and an office were completed, and a good three story hotel well on the way toward completion.

When it is remembered that this was accomplished in so short a time, notwithstanding the fact that every particle of material had to be brought from the East, and that, too, over a slow moving railroad, it will be seen that energy and a determined will were at work.

We should have mentioned sooner that when the point at which to locate the shipping yards was determined upon, a man well versed in the geography of the country and accustomed to life on the prairie, was sent into Southern Kansas and the Indian Territory with instructions to hunt up every straggling drove possible (and every drove was straggling, for they had not where to go) and tell them of Abilene, and what was being done there toward making a market and outlet for Texan cattle. Mounting his pony at Junction City, a lonely ride of almost two hundred miles was taken in a southwesterly direction, crossing the Arkansas River at the site of the present city of Wichita, thence far down into the Indian country; then turning east until trails of herds were found, which were followed until the drove was overtaken, and the owner fully posted in that, to him, all-absorbing topic, to-wit: a good, safe place to drive to, where he could sell or ship his cattle unmolested to other markets.

This was joyous news to the drover, for the fear of trouble and violence hung like an incubus over his waking thoughts alike with his sleeping moments. It was almost too good to be believed; could it be possible that some one was about to afford a Texan drover any other reception than outrage and robbery? They were very suspicious that some trap was set, to be sprung on them; they were not ready to credit the proposition that the day of fair dealing had dawned for Texan drovers, and the era of mobs, brutal murder, and arbitrary proscription ended forever.

Yet they turned their herds toward the point designated, and slowly and cautiously moved on northward, their minds constantly agitated with hope and fear alternately.

## The First Herds

The first herd that arrived at Abilene was driven from Texas by a Mr. Thompson, but sold to Smith, McCord & Chandler, Northern men, in the Indian Nation, and by them driven to Abilene. However, a herd owned by Colonel O.W. Wheeler, Wilson and Hicks, all Californians, en route for the Pacific States, were stopped about thirty miles from Abilene for rest, and finally disposed of at Abilene, was really the first herd that came up from Texas, and broke the trail, followed by the other herds. About thirty-five thousand head were driven in 1867.

It should be borne in mind that it was fully the first of July before it was decided to attempt a cattle depot at Abilene or elsewhere, which, of course, was too late to increase the drive from Texas that year, but time enough only to gather together at that point such herds as were already on the road northward. Not until the cattle were nearly all at Abilene would the incredulous K.P. Railway Company build the requisite switch, and then not until a written demand was made for it, after which, an order was issued to put in a twenty-car switch, and particular direction was given to use "cull" ties, adding that they expected to take it up next year. It was with great difficulty that a hundred car switch was obtained instead of the twenty-car one. Nor were the necessary transfer and feed yards at Leavenworth put in until plans were made and a man to superintend their construction furnished by the same parties that were laboring so hard to get their enterprise on foot at Abilene. But in a comparatively brief time all things were ready for the shipment of the first train.

As we have before stated, about 35,000 head of cattle arrived at Abilene in 1867. In 1860 we believe that the United States Census gave Texas 3,500,000 head of cattle. We are not sure that this is correct, but believe it is.

## Hardships and Celebration
The drive of 1867 was about one per cent of the supply. Great hardships attended driving that year on account of Osage Indian troubles, excessive rain-storms, and flooded rivers. The cholera made sad havoc with many drovers, some of whom died with the malady and many suffered greatly. The heavy rains caused an immense growth of grass, too coarse and washy to be good food for cattle or horses, and but little of the first years' arrivals at Abilene

were fit to go to market. However, on the 5th of September, 1867, the first shipment of twenty cars was made to Chicago. Several Illinois stock men and others, joined in an excursion from Springfield, Ill., to Abilene, to celebrate by feast, wine and song, the auspicious event.

Arriving at Abilene in the evening, several large tents, including one for dining purposes, were found ready for the reception of guests. A substantial repast was spread before the excursionists, and devoured with a relish peculiar to camp life, after which wine, toasts, and speechifying were the order until a late hour at night.

Before the sun had mounted high in the heavens on the following day, the iron horse was darting down the Kaw Valley with the first train load of cattle that ever passed over the Kansas Pacific Railroad, the precursor to many thousands destined to follow.

# An Early Account of Western Rail Travel

*Helen Hunt Jackson*

For several years after it was first completed, the transcontinental railroad captured the public imagination. With the new western railroads, Americans could now cross the nation in a matter of days rather than weeks. Helen Hunt Jackson was an author and traveler who wrote of her experiences on the Union Pacific in the early 1870s. The novelty and excitement of rail travel is evident in her account.

As you read, consider the following questions:
1. Does Jackson seem upset by the hectic nature of rail travel?
2. What different types of train passengers does the author describe?
3. How does Jackson describe the "old emigrant road" that settlers followed before the coming of the railroads?

---

We cross the Missouri at Council Bluffs; begin grumbling at the railroad corporations for forcing us to take a transfer train across the river; but find ourselves plunged into the confusion of Omaha before we have finished railing at the confusion of her neighbor. Now we see for the first time the distinctive expression of American overland travel. Here all luggage is weighed and rechecked for points further west. An enormous shed is filled with it. Four and five deep stand the anxious owners, at a high wooden wall, behind which nobody may go. Everybody holds up checks, and gesticulates and beckons.

Excerpted from *Bits of Travel at Home*, by Helen Hunt Jackson (Boston: Roberts Brothers, 1878).

There seems to be no system; but undoubtedly there is. Side by side with the rich and flurried New-Yorker stands the poor and flurried emigrant. Equality rules. Big bundles of feather-beds, tied up in blue check, red chests, corded with rope, get ahead of Saratoga trunks. Many languages are spoken. German, Irish, French, Spanish, a little English, and all varieties of American, I heard during thirty minutes in that luggage-shed. Inside the wall was a pathetic sight,— a poor German woman on her knees before a chest, which had burst open on the journey. It seemed as if its whole contents could not be worth five dollars,—so old, so faded, so coarse were the clothes and so battered were the utensils. But it was evidently all she owned; it was the home she had brought with her from the Fatherland, and would be the home she would set up in the prairie. The railroad-men were good to her, and were helping her with ropes and nails. This comforted me somewhat; but it seemed almost a sin to be journeying luxuriously on the same day and train with that poor soul.

## Everybody Was Busy

"Lunches put up for people going West." This sign was out on all corners. Piles of apparently ownerless bundles were stacked all along the platforms; but everybody was too busy to steal. Some were eating hastily, with looks of distress, as if they knew it would be long before they ate again. Others, wiser, were buying whole chickens, loaves of bread, and filling bottles with tea. Provident Germans bought sausage by the yard. German babies got bits of it to keep them quiet. Murderous-looking rifles and guns, with strapped rolls of worn and muddy blankets, stood here and there; murderous, but jolly-looking miners, four-fifths boots and the rest beard, strode about, keeping one eye on their weapons and bedding. Well-dressed women and men with polished shoes, whose goods were already comfortably bestowed in palace-cars, lounged up and down, curious, observant, amused. Gay placards, advertising all possible routes; cheerful placards, setting forth the advantages of travellers' insurance policies; insulting placards, assuming that all travellers have rheumatism, and should take "Unk Weed;" in short, just such placards as one sees everywhere,—papered the walls. But here they seemed somehow to be true and merit attention, especially the "Unk Weed." There is such a professional croak in that first syllable; it sounds as if the weed had a diploma.

"All aboard!" rung out like the last warning on Jersey City wharves when steamers push off for Europe; and in the twinkling of an eye we were out again in the still, soft, broad prairie, which is certainly more like sea than like any other land.

## The Ride

Again flowers and meadows, and here and there low hills, more trees, too, and a look of greater richness. Soon the Platte River, which seems to be composed of equal parts of sand and water, but which has too solemn a history to be spoken lightly of. It has been the silent guide for so many brave men who are dead! The old emigrant road, over which they went, is yet plainly to be seen; at many points it lies near the railroad. Its still, grass-grown track is strangely pathetic. Soon it will be smooth prairie again, and the wooden headboards at the graves of those who died by the way will have fallen and crumbled.

Dinner at Fremont. The air was sharp and clear. The disagreeable guide-book said we were only 1,176 feet above the sea; but we believed we were higher. The keeper of the dining-saloon apologized for not having rhubarb-pie, saying that he had just sent fifty pounds of rhubarb on ahead to his other saloon. "You'll take tea there to-morrow night."

"But how far apart are your two houses?" said we.

"Only eight hundred miles. It's considerable trouble to go back an' forth, an' keep things straight; but I do the best I can."

Two barefooted little German children, a boy and girl, came into the cars here, with milk and coffee to sell. The boy carried the milk, and was sorely puzzled when I held out my small tumbler to be filled. It would hold only half as much as his tin measure, of which the price was five cents.

"Donno's that's quite fair," he said, when I gave him five cents. But he pocketed it, all the same, and ran on, swinging his tin can and pint cup, and filling out, "Nice fresh milk. Last you'll get! No milk any further west." Little rascal! We found it all the way; plenty of it too, such as it was. It must be owned, however, that sage-brush and prickly pear (and if the cows do not eat these, what do they eat?) give a singularly unpleasant taste to milk; and the addition of alkali water does not improve it.

# The Railroad Encourages Settlement of the West

*George A. Batchelder*

The boundaries of the contiguous United States were largely defined in 1845, when Mexico ceded California, New Mexico, Nevada, Utah, and Texas to the United States in the Treaty of Guadalupe-Hidalgo. But only after the western railroads were built did many of the Southwestern and Midwestern territories—including Colorado, North and South Dakota, Montana, Idaho, Wyoming, Utah, Oklahoma, New Mexico, and Arizona—achieve statehood.

The railroads made it easier for settlers to go west than ever before. In the 1870s the eastern seaboard was flooded with propaganda encouraging western migration. These pamphlets, books, and other promotional materials were published by the railroad companies themselves as well as western land speculators and other interested parties. In this excerpt from a book encouraging settlement of the Dakota Territory, the author emphasizes that the railroads have made it easier than ever before for pioneers to start a new life in the West.

As you read, consider the following questions:
1. Why should young men go west, in the author's opinion?
2. How does Batchelder describe the population growth in the Dakota Territory and in Minnesota?
3. What effect will the railroads have on the Dakotas, according to the author?

Excerpted from *A Sketch of the History and Resources of Dakota Territory*, by George A. Batchelder (Yankton, SD: Press Steam Power Printing Company, 1870).

Think of it young men, you who are "rubbing" along from year to year, with no great hopes for the future, can you accept for a little while the solitude of nature and bear a few hard knocks for a year or two? Lay aside your paper collars and kid gloves. Work a little. Possess your soul with patience and hold on your way with a firm purpose. Do this, and there is a beautiful home for you out here. Prosperity, freedom, independence, manhood in its highest sense, peace of mind and all the comforts and luxuries of life are awaiting you. The fountain of perennial youth is in the country, never in the city. Its healing, beautifying and restoring waters do not run through aqueducts. You must lie down on the mossy bank beneath trees, and drink from gurgling brooks and crystal streams.

Nine out of every ten young men without fortune in Boston and elsewhere, have high hopes for the future. They are going to do something by and by. When they get on a little farther they will show us what they can accomplish; but the chances are they never get that little farther on. The tide is against them. We are liable to forget that we measure ourselves by what we are going to do, whereas the world estimates us by what we have already done.

The young man who has measured off ribbon several years, in all probability is doing no better to-day than he was five years ago; and will be no farther along, except in years, five years hence than he is now.

## A New Society

How can any young man of spirit settle himself down to earning a bare existence, when all this vast region of the Northwest, with its boundless, undeveloped resources before him, is inviting him on? They will be nobodies where they are—they can be somebodies in building up a new society.

Young men predominate in the West, while maidens are scarce; therefore I say to you, get yourself a wife and bring her with you. You will be happier and more contented, and, I have no doubt, make money faster.

To young women I would say just a word. Out here

"There is no goose so gray,
   but, soon or late,
Will find some honest gander
   for a mate."

Therefore, attach yourself to some family emigrating, and if you are over 21 years, your 160 acres of land, to which you are entitled, and your other attractions, will soon find you a nest and a mate.

The West grows apace—more rapidly than you in the East get an idea of. It is said that, like a pumpkin vine, you can almost see it grow. Emigration travels fast. As fires blown by winds sweep through the dried grass of the prairies, so civilization spreads along the frontier.

Nine years ago the site of Yankton was covered with Indian lodges where now stand 400 houses with 2,000 inhabitants.

Our next neighbor east, the State of Minnesota, the future central state of the future American Continental Republic, twenty years ago had scarcely a population of five thousand, and now has over half a million. Eighteen years ago her whole total valuation in real and personal property was eight hundred thousand dollars, and now it is considerably over one hundred millions of dollars, and yet only about one-hundredth part of her area under cultivation. Think of the future and measure it by the advancement already made.

It is undoubtedly hard for many persons who would like to come West, to pull up their stakes in their own homes, and cut loose from old associations, and strike out alone upon the prairie. The human race is gregarious and prefers society to solitude, therefore I would advise the emigration of families together. Coming as a colony they will bring the moral atmosphere of their old homes with them. Within a week of their arrival they will have established a school and a church, and on a Sunday morning will ascend, yet lingering on the summer air, sweeter than the lays of birds amid the flowers, the songs of the Sunday school established in their new home. . . .

It is the glory of our civilization that it adapts itself to all the circumstances of life.

The future of Dakota is not chimerical. Utah, Kansas and Nebraska have magnificent prairies and an exceedingly fertile soil, but they lack moisture. There are no rivers, ponds, wood-fringed lakes or gurgling brooks. In contrast to this is the domain of the great Northwest. For a few years the tide of emigration may flow, as it does now, into the more central States; but when the lands there along the rivers and streams are taken up, the great river of human life setting toward the Pacific, will be turned up the Missouri, the Red River of the North and the rivers of that country on and near the Northern Pacific Railroad.

## "Dakota Will Have Her Railroads"

Formerly the individual was the pioneer of civilization; now, the railroad is the pioneer, and the individual follows, or is only slightly in advance. Before the flowers bloom another year, Dakota will have her railroads; they will bring more towns, villages, churches, school houses, newspapers, and thousands of new and free people. The wild roses are blooming today, and the sod is yet unturned, and the prairie chicken rears her brood in quiet and safety, where, in a year or two will be heard the screech of the locomotive and the tramp of the approaching legions, another year will bring the beginning of the change; towns and cities will spring into existence, and the steam whistle and the noise of saws and hammers, and the click and clatter of machinery, the sound of industry will be heard. The prairies will be golden with the ripening harvest, and the field and the forest, the mine and the river, will all yield their abundance to the ever growing multitude.

# CHRONOLOGY

## 1787
On July 13 Congress passes the Northwest Ordinance, which sets guidelines for settlement of the western frontier.

## 1803
In April, France agrees to sell the Louisiana Territory to the United States for $15 million. On August 13 Meriwether Lewis and William Clark begin their expedition to discover a direct water route across the continent.

## 1806
Zebulon Pike sets out on an expedition to trace the source of the Mississippi River and instead discovers the peak that bears his name. On September 23 Lewis and Clark return to St. Louis, Missouri.

## 1808
John Jacob Astor founds the American Fur Company.

## 1812
The United States and Great Britain clash in the War of 1812, which ends with the Treaty of Ghent on December 24, 1814.

## 1817
Construction of the Erie Canal begins in New York. The canal will become a significant artery in the westward movement of Americans from the East Coast.

## 1820
Explorer Stephen Long leads an expedition across Kansas to the Rocky Mountains. He labels the area east of the Rockies "the Great American Desert," steering settlers away from

the region for decades. On February 17 Congress passes the Missouri Compromise, which prohibits slavery north of latitude 36°30'. There are now twelve slave and twelve free states.

## 1821

On January 17 the Spanish governor of Texas grants Moses Austin permission to settle three hundred families in the region. Mexico rebels against Spain and wins independence on August 24 with the signing of the Treaty of Córdoba. In November trader William Becknell blazes the Santa Fe Trail between Independence, Missouri, and Santa Fe, Mexico. The trail becomes the principal avenue for manufactured goods and immigrants bound for Santa Fe and the Southwest.

## 1825

The federal government adopts a policy of exchanging Indian lands in the East for public land in the West and establishes an Indian Territory in the region known as the Great American Desert.

## 1826

Fur trapper Jedediah Smith leads the first party of Americans overland to California.

## 1834

Congress establishes the Department of Indian Affairs.

## 1835

Samuel F.B. Morse invents the telegraph. In October, Texas declares its independence from Mexico; war between Texas and Mexico follows.

## 1837

On March 3 President Andrew Jackson officially recognizes the Republic of Texas.

## 1838

Over eighteen thousand Cherokee are forcibly relocated to Indian Territory from Georgia, Alabama, and Tennessee along the Trail of Tears.

## 1841

Congress passes the Pre-Emption Act to encourage settlement of the frontier. The act gives squatters the right to purchase federal land at a minimum price.

## 1843

Over one thousand settlers participate in the great migration via the Oregon Trail to the Pacific Northwest. It becomes an annual event, with thousands more settlers following each year.

## 1845

On March 1 lame-duck president John Tyler signs a resolution annexing the Republic of Texas. In his March 4 inauguration speech, President James K. Polk calls for the acquisition of Oregon and California as U.S. territories. The phrase *Manifest Destiny* is coined by magazine editor John L. O'Sullivan.

## 1846

On May 13, after a clash between Mexican and U.S. troops along the Rio Grande, the United States declares war on Mexico. The Mexican War continues until February 1848.

## 1847

On April 16 Brigham Young leads a small group to the Great Salt Lake Basin. The following year thousands of Mormons follow and begin building Salt Lake City.

## 1848

On January 24 gold is discovered at Sutter's Mill near Sacramento, California. During the next two years tens of thousands of "Argonauts" journey to California.

## 1849

The Pacific Railroad Company is chartered and begins construction of the first railroad west of the Mississippi River, from St. Louis to Kansas City.

## 1853

In the Gadsden Purchase, Mexico sells the United States a strip of land running along Mexico's northern border between Texas and California for $10 million.

## 1854

Congress approves the Kansas-Nebraska Act, which repeals the Missouri Compromise of 1820. The Republican Party is born out of opposition to the act and to slavery in general.

## 1858

Gold is discovered at Pike's Peak in Colorado. The '59ers pour into the state the following year.

## 1859

The first major silver strike in the United States, the Comstock Lode, is discovered in Nevada.

## 1860

Republican Abraham Lincoln is elected sixteenth president of the United States. In response, South Carolina secedes from the Union.

## 1861

Mississippi, Florida, Alabama, Georgia, Louisiana, and Texas join South Carolina to form the Confederate States of America. The Civil War begins in April with the clash between Confederate and Union troops at Fort Sumter, South Carolina.

## 1862

The Homestead Act is passed, which allows citizens to acquire 160 acres of land in the public domain by settling on them for five years and paying a small fee.

# 1865

The Civil War ends. The Thirteenth Amendment, which abolishes slavery, is ratified.

# 1867

The United States purchases Alaska from Russia for $7 million. The Kansas Pacific Railroad reaches Abilene, Kansas, and the first cattle drive from Texas up the Chisholm Trail to Abilene marks the beginning of the cattle-driving era.

# 1869

On March 10 the first transcontinental railroad is completed as the Union Pacific Railroad joins the Central Pacific Railroad at Promontory Point in the Utah Territory.

# 1871

Congress passes the Indian Appropriations Act, which ends the practice of treating Indian tribes as sovereign nations. Instead, Indians are legally designated as wards of the federal government.

# 1881

The second transcontinental railroad is completed. Helen Hunt Jackson publishes *A Century of Dishonor*, the first detailed examination of the atrocities committed against American Indians.

# 1887

The free delivery of mail is provided in all communities with a population of at least ten thousand.

# 1889

Congress establishes the Oklahoma Territory on unoccupied lands in the Indian Territory, breaking a sixty-year-old pledge to preserve this area exclusively for American Indians. In the Oklahoma land rush on April 22, thousands of settlers stake their claims on almost 2 million acres of land.

## 1890

After the 1890 census, the federal government declares that the frontier is now settled.

## 1896

The discovery of gold at Bonanza Creek, a tributary of the Klondike River near Dawson City, Alaska, sparks the Klondike Stampede, the last great western gold rush.

## 1898

The United States annexes Hawaii. After a short war with Spain, the United States also acquires Cuba, Puerto Rico, Guam, and the Philippine Islands.

# FOR FURTHER RESEARCH

## General Histories of Westward Expansion

Ray Allen Billington, *America's Frontier Heritage*. Albuquerque: University of New Mexico Press, 1974.

———, *The Far Western Frontier, 1830–1860*. New York: Harper & Row, 1956.

———, *Westward to the Pacific: An Overview of America's Westward Expansion*. St. Louis, MO: Jefferson National Expansion Historical Association, 1979.

Ray Allen Billington and Martin Ridge, *Westward Expansion: A History of the American Frontier*. New York: Macmillan, 1982.

Dee Alexander Brown, *Bury My Heart at Wounded Knee: An Indian History of the American West*. New York: Holt, Rinehart, and Winston, 1970.

Thomas D. Clark, *Frontier America: The Story of the Westward Movement*. New York: Scribner's, 1959.

William H. Goetzmann, *Exploration and Empire: The Explorer and the Scientist in the Winning of the American West*. New York: Norton, 1978.

———, *Mountain Men*. Cody, WY: Buffalo Bill Historical Center, 1978.

Robert V. Hine, *The American West: A New Interpretive History*. New Haven, CT: Yale University Press, 2000.

Wilbur R. Jacobs, *Dispossessing the American Indian: Indians and Whites on the Colonial Frontier*. New York: Scribner's, 1972.

Mary Ellen Jones, *Daily Life on the Nineteenth-Century American Frontier*. Westport, CT: Greenwood, 1998.

Nelson Klose, *A Concise Study Guide to the American Frontier*. Lincoln: University of Nebraska Press, 1964.

Gerald F. Kreyche, *Visions of the American West*. Lexington: University Press of Kentucky, 1989.

S.L.A. Marshall, *Crimson Prairie: The Wars Between the United States and the Plains Indians During the Winning of the West*. New York: Scribner's, 1972.

Walter T.K. Nugent, *Into the West: The Story of Its People*. New York: Knopf, 1999.

Arthur King Peters, *Seven Trails West*. New York: Abbeville, 1996.

Dale Van Every, *The Final Challenge: The American Frontier, 1804–1845*. New York: Quill, 1988.

Sanford Wexler, ed., *Westward Expansion: An Eyewitness History*. New York: Facts On File, 1991.

## Collections of Primary Documents

William F. Deverell and Anne F. Hyde, eds., *The West in the History of the Nation: A Reader, Volume One: To 1877*. Boston: Bedford/St. Martin's, 2000.

Robert V. Hine and Edwin R. Bingham, eds., *The Frontier Experience: Readings on the Trans-Mississippi West*. Belmont, CA: Wadsworth, 1963.

Robert W. Richmond and Robert W. Mardock, eds., *A Nation Moving West: Readings in the History of the American Frontier*. Lincoln: University of Nebraska Press, 1966.

## The Lewis and Clark Expedition

Stephen E. Ambrose, *Lewis and Clark: Voyage of Discovery*. Washington, DC: National Geographic Society, 1998.

———, *Undaunted Courage: Meriwether Lewis, Thomas Jefferson, and the Opening of the American West*. New York: Simon & Schuster, 1996.

Frank Bergon, ed., *The Journals of Lewis and Clark*. New York: Penguin, 1989.

Sally Senzel Isaacs, *America in the Time of Lewis and Clark: 1801 to 1850*. Des Plaines, IL: Heinemann Library, 1998.

Donald Jackson, *Thomas Jefferson and the Stony Mountains: Exploring the West from Monticello*. Norman: University of Oklahoma Press, 1993.

Donald Jackson, ed., *Letters of the Lewis and Clark Expedition with Related Documents, 1783–1854*. Chicago: University of Illinois Press, 1978.

Bill and Jan Moeller, *Lewis and Clark: A Photographic Journey*. Missoula, MT: Mountain, 1999.

Daniel P. Thorp, *Lewis and Clark: An American Journey*. New York: MetroBooks, 1998.

## Manifest Destiny

William H. Goetzmann, *When the Eagle Screamed: The Romantic Horizon in American Expansionism*. Norman: University of Oklahoma Press, 2000.

Norman A. Graebner, ed., *Manifest Destiny*. Indianapolis: Bobbs-Merrill, 1968.

Frederick Merk, *Manifest Destiny and Mission in American History: A Reinterpretation*. Westport, CT: Greenwood, 1983.

Robert Sobel, *Conquest and Conscience: The 1840s*. New York: Crowell, 1971.

## The California Gold Rush

Peter J. Blodgett, *Land of Golden Dreams: California in the Gold Rush Decade, 1848–1858*. San Marino, CA: Huntington Library, 1999.

Mary Hill, *Gold: The California Story*. Berkeley and Los Angeles: University of California Press, 1999.

J.S. Holliday, *Rush for Riches: Gold Fever and the Making of California*. Berkeley and Los Angeles: University of California Press, 1999.

Malcolm J. Rohrbough, *Days of Gold: The California Gold Rush and the American Nation*. Berkeley and Los Angeles: University of California Press, 1997.

## The Transcontinental Railroad

Stephen E. Ambrose, *Nothing Like It in the World: The Men Who Built the Transcontinental Railroad, 1863–1869*. New York: Simon & Schuster, 2000.

Dee Alexander Brown, *Hear That Lonesome Whistle Blow*. New York: Simon & Schuster, 1994.

John F. Stover, *American Railroads*. Chicago: University of Chicago Press, 1997.

# INDEX